Father Bill

Reflections of a Beloved Rebel

Edited by Mary O'Donnell

Pacific View Press
Berkeley, Ca

Text copyright © 2009 Mary O'Donnell

Cover design Jos Sances

Interior design Nancy Ippolito

ISBN 978-1-881896-33-3

All rights reserved. No part of this book may be used or reproduced, stored in a retrieval system, or transmitted, in any form or by any means, electronic, mechanical, photocopying, recording, or otherwise without prior permission in writing from the publisher. Address inquiries to Mary O'Donnell, P.O. Box 99844, Emeryville, CA 94662, or at *odonnellmary7@gmail.com*.

Library of Congress Cataloging-in-Publication Data

O'Donnell, Bill, 1930-2003.
  Father Bill : reflections of a beloved rebel / edited by Mary O'Donnell.
    p. cm.
  ISBN 978-1-881896-33-3
  1. Theology. 2. Christianity and justice--Catholic Church. 3. Christian sociology--Catholic Church. I. O'Donnell, Mary. II. Title. III. Title: Reflections of a beloved rebel.
  BX4705.O343A5 2009
  261.8--dc22
                                    2009003483

Printed in the United States

To my children:
Steven, David, Matthew, Carol, and Jeannie
With gratitude and love

Contents

Preface .... *vi*

"The Ballad of Wild Bill" 1

Wisdom 3

Humor 21

Prayer 25

Faith 35

Hope 44

Love 48

Peace 52

Forgiveness 56

Protest and Nonviolence 60

Prison 73

Preface

> He is like a tree planted near
> running water that yields its
> fruit in due season and whose
> leaves never fade.
>
> —Psalm 1:3

He was the second-oldest in a family of seven, born a few minutes before his twin brother Gene. He was known to his friends as "Wild Bill," a tribute to his having been arrested near 300 times in the cause of human rights and doing six months time in a federal penitentiary.

Bill was always available to me, and I was honored to be called his "best friend," and while I can still hear my brother's voice, it is in that spirit I undertook the task of editing a small portion of his writings to continue his legacy as a champion of peace and justice, and to inspire and encourage others in the same work.

My brother, Father Bill was a charismatic Catholic priest, advocate for the poor, for workers, street alcoholics, drug addicts, and a conscience to politicians. A close friend and counselor to numerous prominent activists, his parish, Saint Joseph the Worker, in Berkeley, California, was a refuge for many of them, including United Farm Worker founder Cesar Chavez and actor Martin Sheen. Bill was a true patriot; one who loved his church and country enough to "speak truth to power" and to exhort its leaders to serve the people according to God's will. He enjoined his readers to nonviolent action in the cause of peace and justice. More importantly he walked the talk on picket lines and in numerous protests for over thirty years.

Bill was confident of the possibilities of encountering God: "Nature has created us with the capacity to know God, to experience God, just as it has created us with the capacity to know speech. The experience of God (which is grace) or in any case the possibility of experiencing God, is the innate mystery of God-with-me and I-with-God." For Bill, "belief was not static certitude, but trust in guides on a mysterious journey: by trusting spiritual wisdom and living it, God could be known."

—Mary O'Donnell

Acknowledgements

Deepest gratitude to James O'Donnell, Ed O'Donnell, Jane Sartain, Rosemary Brennan, Father Brian Joyce, Al Garrotto, Kevin Ryan, John Savant, and John Fromer and in memory of Janet Foldvary; also to Saint Patrick's Seminary Alumni Association, Father Stephan Kappler and Saint Joseph's Parish, Sheila Mullen and Bob "Hey Mr. Green" Schildgen and Nancy Ippolito of Pacific View Press.

The Ballad of Wild Bill

By John Fromer

Some used to call him Bill
Some called him the worker priest
Some knew him as a prisoner
Or a friend out on the street.

Worn out jeans and tennis shoes
A motorcycle jacket on his back
The collar of a priest and the joy of a child
Father Bill always made you laugh.

Chorus: He believed in . . .
The power of love and the love of life
The power of the people when we organize
The power of love and the love of life
The power of the people when we organize

A Catholic priest who blest gay marriage
Thought women should be priests
The finest listener and the kindest heart
Found hope by hitting the street

Father Bill fought for the union
Walked the walk on every line
From Alabama and Georgia to the city by the bay
He was arrested more than 200 times.

Chorus: He had . . .

Fort Benning, Georgia, the school of the Assassins
He dared to cross the line
He called the judge a pimp for the Pentagon
Father Bill did six month's time.

Chorus: He had . . .

His church was home to the homeless
A bed where Caesar Chavez would sleep
A place where Muslims, Jews, and Catholics
Are working together for peace

Chorus: He had . . .

The janitors and the teachers, the farmers in the field
The workers in the sweatshops and in the mills
The poor and suffering, and thousands in jail
We will remember Father Bill . . .

Chorus:
He had the power of love and the love of life
The power of the people when we organize
The power of love and the love of life
The power of the people when we organize

Wisdom

Father Bill didn't think of himself as an author, and never took the time to formally publish his work. Aside from a very humble view of his own literary gifts, he was too busy to prepare his work for any press. His days were filled with saying masses, running a parish, counseling addicts and alcoholics, visiting the sick, speaking to unions and other progressive organizations, and protesting against social injustice, war, and nuclear testing and research. (Ironically he grew up on a farm near the Lawrence Livermore Laboratory in Northern California, where he engaged in Good Friday protests each year.) He also served on various boards, including those of a housing cooperative, a recovery program, and several international charitable organizations. He spent a considerable amount of time on delegations visiting other countries to witness firsthand the tragic effects of U.S. foreign policy and to advance peace and alleviation of poverty.

But Bill produced a large volume of writing as part of his duties as a priest: weekly church bulletins and sermons for more than four decades; prayers delivered at both religious and secular events, and, near the end of his life, musings and letters while he was confined to federal prison for trespassing on government property during a protest against the School of the Americas, where the U.S. government trains people in methods of torture and other terrorist techniques.

The writings here are drawn from these sources. They cover a wide range, from Biblical interpretations to reflections on the relation between faith and activism to prayer to pithy observations and favorite jokes. The writing is sometimes sharply critical of official Church policy, but at the same time theologically orthodox. Father Bill had no reservations in criticizing the Church institution and its hierarchy, but did not challenge core doctrines such as the Incarnation or the sacraments of the Church. He saw these ancient teachings as paths to contemplation and fuller experience of the grace of God. For him the existence of God was not in question. The real question was how to enter more deeply into that existence. Bill saw the possibility in traditional terms of losing one's corrupt self in prayer, activism, and openness to others. This meant letting go of trappings of this self that block grace and allowing it to enter one's heart. In wrestling with this basic goal, Bill could be as critical of himself as he was of the institutional Church.

Because spiritual growth depended on our commitment to others, for Bill there could be no individual salvation without communal engagement—or as he put it, "God-like is what God-like does."

It may be folk wisdom not to trust a husband too far and a bachelor too near. If the husband as well as the bachelor completely trust God, then the wife could feel quite safe.

Just ponder this: we exist in God's mind as spirit,
    a being without matter. Then we are conceived into flesh.
        This process can't happen without woman.
        And also is it in the mind of God that this spirit born flesh be "Inspirited" with God; that is to say, that the very spirit of God is to live in the person born.
    This mystery can't happen without our permission and cooperation.
        We have to be willing to go along.
            We have to say along with Mary who said to the angel: "Let it be . . . !"

Reading the Bible of facts, taking it all literally, is crazy-making. For me, and I suspect with most people, reading scripture is the experience of the story peeling away somewhat hidden truths about myself. It's letting the Bible read me.

In the world of sexuality, the cry for moral clarity indicates a moral deafness in the ears of the aging cardinals in such areas as mandatory celibacy, the ordination of women, of gays, and of activating a married clergy like the Greek orthodox and other Christian denominations. The Vatican on birth control is as up-to-date as supporting the flat-earth theory.

As the body can be the dump for slop, so can the soul be a bin for intellectual garbage and ethical toxins. Some examples:

capital punishment protects society;
war wins the peace;
abortion is a free choice;
this is a democracy;
capitalism is the best economic system;
some violence is morally justifiable;
a little greed helps;
humility is a loser, the poor are lazy;
"I can quit anytime";
"she made me hit her";
"my country right or wrong."

There is no end to their unhealthy litany. It even claims to be "reality." That's how spiritually toxic it is.

> Jesus claimed to be the God-Bread, the true soul food. The formula for health is contained in the Sermon on the Mount, the Lord's Prayer, in the parables. The Good News is that we can be healthy forever; the powerful sign and pledge is consuming the God Bread, where God becomes a part of us and we a part of God, and this is evidenced in how we support and serve one another.

If Jesus came in a particular time in history, preached his stunning mountain sermon, healed the hurting, got executed for his big mouth, and then went Bye-Bye, he would have been the biggest So-What of all history. All those good works, wasted and forgotten. No, Jesus intended to be remembered and imitated. That was his chief mandate at the Last Supper. His last act: pass it on, lads. His being born, his poking around and hanging out, his dying, and his rising were precisely so he could be around, down, present, through us, all time and everywhere, forever. Like an eagle he soars.

The heart of the Christian is drawn to the heart of Jesus. Self-discovery is imperative. The only road to God-discovery. Passion in this pursuit makes us leap over barriers.

When there is no self-acceptance there will be self-lying. For anything outside of us can never claim us until it is first owned inwardly.

Being your real self is what Jesus invites us to be. When we are, we see something of the true person that we are.

"Everyone in Hollywood wants to be like Ghandi: thin, tan, and moral." The driven pursuit, of "thin, tan, and moral" (sic) makes a liar out of Jesus Christ when he spoke so brilliantly, yet simply, about the infinite value of bread: "I am the bread of life, whoever comes to me will never hunger, and whoever believes in me will never thirst.

Acting out of the pretending self only limits how great a person can be.

The Journey is letting oneself be who one is, rather than who family, boss, spouse, lover dictates who they are supposed to be. Pretense is the impassible roadblock.

When we are true to ourselves, it seems we are giving permission to other people to be true to themselves. They no longer feel they have to pretend. The free self liberates the trapped self in the other.

"We are the world, we stand together as one. . . . We are all a part of God's great family," so runs a popular song.

We tend not to trust God. What's left but to take over complete control of our own hearts and minds to become our own little Hitlers. If I can't trust God to give me more than I need but more than I want, then that leaves only me to ravage and exploit as much as what I can get away with. I get into barking orders at myself, which quickly gets into barking orders at you.

When we sense apathy at our center, that's a signal we are refusing to pay the cost of "The Pearl of great price."

A person has been in the mind of God
from eternity. A person is a child of God,

a member of God's family. A person is God-like,
reflecting God's glory even more so than
the moon reflects the sun. Unlike an individual,
it's the person who is loved or hated, who is
lovable or not; it's the person who loves or hates.
As an individual I am a human being, just like you, no more
no less. As a person I am Bill O'Donnell;
as a person I am no more like you than I am like
the Pope.

Want to be free? . . . Jesus was saying . . . Expect and even welcome conflict.

They are one when the follower can accept loving one's enemy. Impossible? Of course! Without God's help.
This is the why of Pentecost.
Our hearts are home to the Holy Spirit.
With Her, there is nothing we can't do.

God-like
is
what God-like does.

Evil begets evil, as the cliché goes. A murder
is committed. Or a grievous injury. Revenge
prompts, even demands, getting even. The
only trouble with that, as the Chinese say:
"Who opts for revenge should dig two graves."

Consumerism is one of the three most virulent social diseases worldwide. Another name for the same thing is materialism.

To live wholesomely, we don't need most of the stuff that has come to possess us. Rather than we possess it, stuff has come to possess us.

Who isn't one big bundle of wants and needs?
If I am not, then I'm either dead or a saint, and I am neither one of those. Because of the human condition there is a terrible tension, sometimes springing a war between our wants and needs. Needs crave for what it takes to be alive, from hunger and sex, to name a few, to intellectual curiosity and a craving for beauty. Wants grasp for more, more. Mother Te-

resa quite pointedly said: "It's a very great poverty to decide that a child must die that you might wish to live as you wish."

It's become a killing addiction. Feeling down? Go shopping. But I don't need a new dress or shirt. But it'll make me feel good. Feeling depressed? You need a sugar rush. Nothing like chocolate to satisfy. Fattening? Start my diet tomorrow. Just one more drink. Where's my needle?

How do we recover from our addiction to being unfaithful? A day at a time; loving as best as we can, preferring the good of the other, a day at a time; it's doing it, is how we get it. . . . Covenanting, a day at a time.

The challenge is to see ourselves as persons; each is more than an individual, conceived, born, lives and dies—more than an individual who can be categorized: More than this, we are persons. Take a nondescript, colorless, shapeless, simple seed; that's individual. Water, sun, and soil make it a part of nature; it belongs. Then it blooms; a flower or a fruit emerges; in that sense it's like a person, unique, singular, and can never be replaced.

> The story of human suffering is told in the
> twelve-hour drama written and told in the
> Passion of Jesus. The humiliation and degradation,
> the betrayal and cruelty; innocence prejudged,
> condemned and executed, all called "good news"
> because in the end Jesus is victorious,
> as he gave purpose to all pain, suffering, and death,
> for it all ends in life that never ends.

To honor the "God who so loved the world that he gave his only Son, etc.," is to honor his being particularly Jewish. Rather than we making Jesus American, Americans have to identify with being Jewish. That's how we all become catholic. If Jesus is a man for all seasons, so is being Jewish and American and African and Asian for all seasons. Recognizing and acknowledging humanity in diversity is precisely what makes Jesus and all of us universal. It is what makes us Christ-like. Otherwise we are using cosmetics to make over Jesus into our image and likeness; not exactly what God intended or indeed willed.

As hinted at previously, needs and wants sometimes are but the two sides of the same coin. A common mantra on a labor picket line might be: "No justice, no peace." It's saying, we need justice and want peace. In truth commissions established in nations after their civil war, their prefaces read: "There will be no healing without justice, no justice without truth; no truth without full accountability." When these wants and needs are satisfied, then forgiveness may flow, the ultimate act of genuine love.

> It's impossible to live a faithful life . . . but it is not impossible to struggle to live a faithful life . . . and we keep trying and keep doing it over and over again until we get it right . . . or die trying . . . that's what Jesus is telling us . . .
>
> God never gives up; then why should we?

Socrates, one of the fathers of Greek philosophy, was known for his frugal way of living. But he used to love to hang out in what would be malls today. A friend spotted him one day studying intensely some article of clothing and wondered, since ol' Soc never bought anything, why did he so obviously enjoy the marketplace so much?

The great thinker replied: " I am always amazed to see just how many things there are that I don't need!"

A priest at Mass noticed a woman who never missed receiving Communion. She was always accompanied by a man who never received. Father wondered out loud to her about this. "Oh, he's my mentally challenged son and has never received his First Holy Communion!" "That need not ever be a barrier," replied the priest. "Let me give him some preparation and next Sunday he can accompany you to Communion." She was delighted. Next Sunday the young man came to the priest with his mother at his side; he took the host into the palm of his hand, looked at the priest and said, "Thank you!" Then broke the bread and handed a half to his mother.

Certainly a candidate for membership in the Good Shepherds' Global Village.

The family is the building block of society. The world is but a collection of nations; a nation is but a collection of tribes; a tribe is but a collection of clans; a clan is but a collection of kinfolk, and kin is but a collection of families. When the family is not together, then the world is not together. When all of this is not working, then the individual, one's person, is subject to being torn apart. So why does the church make the Jesus, Mary, and Joseph family a model for us who are products of dysfunctional families: and if you don't think so, denial is a sure sign of dysfunctionality. It's embarrassingly simple; they are only holy because they made God the center of their family. Whatever happened to them, they trusted that God was with them, and would never abandon them. That is what bonded them so closely. Because of that relationship, they had to live for others. Their identity depended on it. That leads to dying for others. And that leads to rising so that we, as dysfunctional as we are, may too rise from the ashes of our self-destructive passions. As individuals are sacred, so it follows must families be.

It's a given that the person is not only sacred but also social. How we organize our society—in economics and politics, in law and policy—directly affects human dignity and the capacity of individuals to grow in community. The family is the core, the cell, the central social institution that must be supported and strengthened and never undermined. The belief is that all peoples have that basic right, and it necessarily follows the people's duty to participate in the building of society, pursuing together the common good and well-being of all, especially the poor and vulnerable.

> There's one thing God insists on: not excluding anybody from his party. People decline God's invite because they don't want to associate with "those" people who dress differently, talk differently, don't have "our" values, and are of a different color. People prefer not to attend because "they" are not "our" class of people; or it's "those" people's politics that I can't stand. Their idea of God's party is joining the country club.

Families oblivious to justice are self-destructive.

Jesus Christ is a grace. How else would we know of God's passionate love for us, God's need for us, and our need to reflect that grace onto others. Life dies without grace. With grace we can endure anything, even the prospect of our own death.

> The reign of God is like that moment of ecstasy when time stops. Everything in life stops and you

> know you are loved, you know you will live for ever . . .

God sees you and me as we actually are. God can't help but love us, for God is love. Because God sees us and the three persons of the Trinity in his aloneness, God know us.

The heart of faith in Christ is accepting to be true the ineffably loving and forgiving presence of God in the smallest particle of matter, at the rim of the universe and The Lover whose home is in our hearts.

Prostitutes and tax collectors admit that they are liars; it's part of doing business; being truthful about their business gets them closer to God than pretending to be religious.

> A humble conscience can only prefer what is good and true and just, incapable of choosing anything that would destroy or kill. Given our capacity for temptation, there are probably more proud consciences around than humble. Church's mission is to help us do our best.

>> Jesus didn't ask his friends to tell him what a great man he was for all those healings, feedings, and life restorings he did.
>> Jesus was asking: how well
>> have I revealed what God is like?

Jesus recognizes that to prize reconciliation above conflict is a great temptation; as is preferring peace above justice; tranquility above truth, and security above freedom.

Blood is finally the symbol for soul, the life principle.
It is soul that brings and keeps us alive; where there is no soul, there is no life.

When Jesus talked about his kingdom, he was not envisioning some kind of a distant Shangri-la, some Disney World, or a trip to Nirvana land. He came to show us how to deal with conflict, equipping us with the weapons of nonviolence and love of the enemy, the only hope for overcoming any domination-system.

Like the keystone, Jesus is the reference point of any major decision that has to be made. Paying attention to the keystone, Jesus. Consulting your center, is it right? Is it wrong? As you look at another person, the question becomes how would Jesus relate to the other in this circumstance? Is Jesus the keystone of this community? Is Jesus the reference point when this community decides on an action, or decides not to cooperate in what Jesus would have nothing to do with?

Any kingdom needs a king; Jesus declares a kingdom where there is no right nor left, nor top; no ladder with rungs as in the wealthiest nation in the world that brags of the highest standard of living. Jesus has instead proclaimed a center where all are equal, where none are hungry or thirsty or are strangers, or go naked or sick; and where the violent are converted to nonviolence, or are not a part of the community. This begins when community has the respect that the king does—the kind of king who dies for his people.

Jesus is saying to his disciples, "The world is ours; make it the way I showed you how." "I am with you until the end of the world." "I've ascended into your world; come be with me; come join me in this new and exciting nonviolent revolution."

Religiosity, never religion, is the opium of the people; true faith is the force that exalts the lowly and brings down the proud, that feeds the hungry, that says the poor shall inherit the earth.

Blessed are the refugees, messengers of truth, because they come to us as the grace that opens our hearts.

Blessed are you who see one another as bonded as sister and brother. The Blessed are not only personally responsible for the misuse of God's natural blessings and resources, but for the political, social, and economic structures that cause poverty, injustice, and violence.

God created us and made us organizers of our lives and of nature. In Jesus, God did it again. God made Jesus the light of the world, the salt of the earth, and the yeast of human life. Then Jesus invited people like us, and he invites us to the light, the salt, and the yeast; invites the likes of us to turn this garbage dump of a world, these killing fields, this polluted culture, into the reign of God.

Consider these facts on distribution of resources: a child born into an average American family will use up to 50 times as much of the earth's goods—and leave that much more waste—as a child born into a poor family in the so-called developing world (where it's estimated 88 million of the 92 million people added to the world will be born this year).

So what is this Earth like under our stewardship that Jesus is so totally present in? The story goes that two men were fighting over a piece of land, with each claiming ownership (how typical of us). They both agreed to put their case before the rabbi to resolve. Both men made strong arguments for their respective sides. Said the rabbi, "Since I cannot decide in favor of either of you, let's ask the land!" Putting his ear to the ground, then straightening up, he pronounced his verdict; "Gentlemen, the land says that she belongs to neither of you—but that you belong to her."

> In democratic countries the culture expects its citizens to love their country, but not necessarily their government. This is why elections, fair ones, are so essential for this government to work. In the U.S. and other types of republics, dissent is even encouraged, in order to accomplish a true consensus on how citizens wish to govern themselves. Everyone needs basic rights to be respected and never violated, the right to life and all those rights that it takes to realize a full life, such as clean air, pure water, nutritious food, healing medicine, decent housing, healthy recreation, creative work, soul-enhancing education. If government does not set this as its priority, then it needs reforming; if it resists reforming, then it deserves revolution.

Corporate America's like one giant casino where bleary-eyed managers gamble, enthralled and mesmerized by the entertainment, games, and information, and risk all that is vital, alive, and human in our world on the chance that the big payoff will come, and Technology will finally solve all of our problems. Technology will make us rich, will bring peace and inner harmony. From such a drunk, organizing is the worker's recovery program.

Our culture puts down the importance of friendships, putting in its place things like "quality time," which is technology's double speak for real intimacy and connection. The television has become the family hearth. Computers and videos, the family mentors. Fast food the family meal.

Altogether the world is in the hands of the not altogether able. Only the spirit can bring to perfection all our failures, incompetence, and unfitness. Grinding poverty, not the voluntary kind, distracts, triggering terrible and bitter resentments; however, not as severely as wealth can distract from love.

> There's something anti-human, indeed unnatural,
> about borders and boundaries, invisible from
> outer space, that makes connecting with others
> very difficult.
>> To see and feel the earth as a living
>> organism suggests that we live-ons are her
>> gardeners and stewards.

The greatest threat to our democratic system is from within and not from without, as from terrorist attacks. Corporate America, whose wealth has been buying the seats in Congress and state legislatures, takes the power of self-government from the hands of The People.

The Church has to dream the future, i.e., imagine what it all could be like. The ancients warned us in Proverbs: "Without a vision, we shall perish." Our Church is consumed by our culture, gulliverized by status. Easier to conform than reform. Our addiction to materialism screams for recovery. Like "alkies" in a 12-step program we have to acknowledge our bloated, morally bankrupt status like in "Hello, I'm a recovering Catholic," beginning to meet our souls, clean and clear, for the first time, knowing God there, and meeting God in genuine community.

> As for the First World, it must be said
> most decidedly that our social systems
> are not operating for the benefit of everybody.
> All the "Powers That Be," that they are all fallen
> without exception is a recognizable fact.
> Falseness is not the last word either.

> We believe that these Powers That Be can be redeemed. What has fallen in time can be redeemed in time.

The churches must call on all to serve everyone for the general welfare, excluding no one.

God does not call corporations to make profit, but to make human life more human. Profit can never be an end but only a means.

The Kingdom of God is the principal message in the gospels. Even throughout the Bible, God is the king. King David submitted to God. Jesus' kingdom is always near and available and should be yearned for. Believing Jesus to be "the way, the truth, and the light" is living out God's kingdom.

> God can't help but will that all things exist; otherwise all would disappear into nothingness; this means everything, the cosmos, nature, objects; this applies to history, to institutions, to group as well as to individuals.
> God's Kingdom is as broad and as overarching as God's will is. Meaning that the Kingdom of God is not something other than God—but the Kingdom is God.
> And thus it is the Church is not the kingdom; its mission is to proclaim it as God's own. Our call is to be ready to accept God being present to us and the world.
> We are to be open, alert and sensitive to God's whisperings. Listening intently as we can, then obedience to God's call becomes quite desirous.
> As in life so with God, we must show up, attend to all around us, especially the poor and powerless, then respond by seeking and living this Truth.

The church's mission is to liberate humans from sin, meaning sin as defined by recent popes and councils, such as social and economic injustice, oppression, and the will to dominate by violence that maintains injustice. The church must prophesy and teach; expose sin wherever it finds it, condemn it for what it is. Also educate those enslaved and blinded by sin—both the oppressed and the oppressor—to their human dignity and freedom.

"En-Thused"—August 24, 2003

To be alive we must depend on the outside invading our inside. A fetus is fed by the mother supplying nutrients. On growing up, more sophisticated input is required to become alive. Simple eating and drinking when hungry and thirsty does often affect our mood. Recall that good feeling pulling away from the table in contrast to when we pulled up to that table. Ingesting food and drink makes the moment a little better. Severe diabetics depend on their daily injecting, that boost they get from insulin intake. Medically, numerous are the many varieties of pills and needle injections offered by the pharmaceutical industry to patients for what ails them in order to stay alive. We heart patients know that drill only too well. Mathematicians and scientists are so encouraged by their solutions and discoveries that they are encouraged (injecting heart) to further their pursuits. Intellectual stimulation is as needed as much as the lungs need air. That is the purpose of a teacher, to instill curiosity. Emotionally who doesn't need an uplift when feeling frumpy? The healthiest way is when another offers encouragement to overcome what might seem insurmountable. Lovers when apart suffer the doldrums, until they meet and share. Then all seems right with their world again until forced to leave. Whenever confronted with beauty, especially suddenly, it may be a person, a painting, a piece of nature, a mountain, or the crash of waves washing the rocks and sand at the beach, your breath does a quick inhale of delight.

At this point the reader may well wonder where is this all going? What's the point? In defense, Aristotle believed that the best method of teaching is to go from the known to the unknown. Up until now I have covered what you know already and where I go with this you could well be more knowledgeable than I ever will be. But there is risk in every human endeavor. Here goes. This has been all a lead-up to today's gospel line where Jesus unequivocally says: "It is the spirit that gives life . . . The words I have spoken to you are Spirit and life."

The Greeks had a word for God being infused into one's soul life: "enthusiasm," from Theos: meaning God and you guess what "en" stands for, God entering, influencing, injecting, stimulating, invading, intruding, busting in, God present in the soul. The person becomes "enthused" with God, alive with God. Mary on visiting Elizabeth could claim: "My soul magnifies the Lord." Our culture substitutes "the flesh" with the spirit. An Irishman after touring the country was asked his impression of America. His response was characteristically blunt: "Your culture seems to dictate that whatever you can't eat, drink, wear, or screw, it's no damn good, throw it away." The culture in Jesus' day was probably quite similar. He said: "Worshiping the flesh is to no avail." Arnie as in Schwarzenegger has evolved from the flesh when his body was adored as "Mr. Universe" when younger. Now he resorts to the world of politics. At least it's a move toward the spirit; however, if it's a good spirit or a bad spirit, only if he is elected governador will we know. That the "Word" can be twisted, distorted and manipulated is another theme to be taken up some time again. Jesus is making love to his people when he announces that without God coming from the outside and entering into you to turn you on, or to "enthuse" you. To deny God a home is to end up as dust to be blown away in the storms of history. —The OD

Ego lets us imagine we are different,
                superior, better than.

Humility invites us to recover our original unity. Humility leads us to discover what we have to be is actually what we already are. Jesus dares to tell the world that without humility there is no humanity, or "Whoever wishes to be great among you will be your servant, whoever wishes to be first among us will be the slave of all."

Humility is looking into the mirror to gauge our true selves, owning our weakness and faults, our excesses, and vanities, our need to be a little above, if not #1.

Humility is recovering our oneness with the other. That other may only seem to be quite different, and yet seeing beyond the mirror it reveals how we basically are all equal and the same in our humanity.

Humility is unraveling that ego that twists and distorts our vision into our true selves, and the true self of the other.

Humility is the knockout punch to envy and jealousy. Humility demands respect for the other's inviolate body; as well as for one's own.

Humility commands us to eat and drink healthily.

Humility buries arrogance and lets equality bind one to the other.

Humility opens our eyes to see that we are all already one.

Liberation Theology—October 5, 2003.

The oppressed struggle to be free with God's help . . . Out of the poor's economic desperation in Latin America, educators in the 1960s began producing a theology of liberation, defining anew peacemaking for the majority of the world's Catholics. Leaders such as Gutierrez, Boff, Segundo, and Freire rejected the dualism of Plato, a European tradition that splits into an inner, pietistic spirituality and a neutral or indeed a hostile attitude toward the world. Following Vatican II's direction they embraced the integration of the individual and of the world. Personal salvation and that of the world is as one. Liberation theologians put less emphasis on traditional doctrine, conventional spirituality and liturgical devotion—or orthodoxy (right teaching)—than on the visible imitation of Christ in the world and the life of committed love and justice—or orthopraxis (right behavior).

Like the Renaissance Humanists, e.g., Erasmus, and the medieval mendicants, e.g., the Franciscans, their emphasis is not on the intellectual and individualistic aspects of piety and salvation, but on the ethical demands of the gospel: the calling of each Christian to live the Mountain Sermon, to build God's domination (free order), not only for the afterlife but concretely to pursue social justice and peace here and now.

Liberation Theology teaches that the world and its history are one; the church is neither above nor outside this history; instead the church is the sacrament of the world, the vanguard rather for God's Kingdom. As such it cannot act as an institution protecting a privileged position in the world, but must act as the chief agency of liberation, not only for its immediate members, but for all of God's creation.

Liberation Theology's vision is on end times, looking at the "signs of the times" in hopes of the "New Age" solidarity with all persons. The process is called: "conscientization," uniting the slave and master as equals in God's world.

The Bible is the inspiration of Liberation Theology, from the Exodus story to Christ, announcing his mission in Luke 4:1–3: "good news to the poor, release to the captives, sight to the blind, liberty to the oppressed, etc." His desert temptations are models for rejecting materialism, power, and despair. Church people must embrace hope and bring the "good news" not to the rich, the powerful, and the comfortable, but to the marginal, the outcasts, and those who can, will to see the truth, known as "preferential option for the poor."

At the core of this revolution of Liberation Theology is nonviolent direct action; this struggle necessitates conflict—conflict forces choices—to dialogue, negotiations, agreements, or rejection, exile, jailing, and death. Opting to struggle is the call. Victory is only accidental. Choosing the cross before resurrection frees one to be fully human, which mirrors God's glory.

A simple way to remember the essence of Liberation Theology is to picture a five-pointed star; the center presenting God and God's world. Each point of the star representing what the people do: The first point represents PRAYER in its various forms, from meditation to Eucharist. The second point is GIVING, sharing from intellect to goods. The third point is FORGIVING, core to moving ahead. Revenge stalls. The fourth point is JUSTICE where respect is practiced. The fifth point of the star is COMMUNITY. Living L.T. guarantees PEACE. . . . —The OD

Humor

Father Bill often emphasized the point that the gospels teach us to live life to the fullest—to enjoy. One of Bill's great joys was a hearty laugh, and his laughter often brought out the sense of humor in others. His irrepressible Irish sense of humor encompassed every imaginable kind of joke, including some very risqué material. The following is a sample of some of the humor he enjoyed.

Father Bill received a black shirt for his birthday. The sender undoubtedly thought it an appropriate gift for a priest. Bill wrote back, "Now the Mafia will accept me."

Bill said, "I heard Walter Johnson speak many times: I know a wise man when I hear him; or at least he told me he was! Recently I went to Walter for advice; "Walter," I complained, "it's hard being a Catholic priest and all, with having to fight conservative parishioners and priests, with Rome, looking over your shoulder all the time. Walter, I said, I think I'm losing my faith: what do you think I ought to do?"

"No problem," Walter answered, "You can become a Lutheran, just like I am!"

"Walter," I said, "I may be losing my faith, but I'm not losing my mind!"

It was confirmation time for the young people in this church.

The pastor, proud of his having prepared the children and wanting to show them off in front of the Bishop and their parents, had them all assembled in their Sunday best and with the Bishop presiding opened up the ceremony with an inquisition.

Father asked his brightest student the catechism question: "What is the state of matrimony?"

Susie answered, "Matrimony is a state of terrible torment, which those who enter are compelled to undergo for a time, to prepare them for a better world."

Humiliated, the pastor chided Susie: "No, no, no. That's not the state of matrimony. That's the state of Purgatory!"

The Bishop interrupted: "Susie, for someone so young, you have very deep insights."

> Here's food for laughs provided by catechists whose students offered the following answers to catechism quiz:
>
> Lot's wife was a pillar of salt by day and a ball of fire by night.
>
> David fought the Kinkelsteins, a race of people who lived in biblical times.
>
> Paul preached acrimony, which is another name for marriage.
>
> The epistles were the wives of the apostles.
>
> Jesus was born because Mary had an immaculate contraption.

When this Pope died, the whole world mourned, so popular and beloved was he. Thus it became incumbent upon St. Peter to give Pope William a special welcome. "Enter without delay and of course you have access to every part of heaven, and because of your exemplary life on earth you need make no appointment to see our Founder any time. Is there anything Pope Bill may desire?" "As a matter of fact there is. Could I see the original transcripts of the conversations that went on between God and the prophets...What was actually said?" Peter gestured generously: "The whole library of Heaven is yours." Much later a terrifying scream of anguish seared the library stacks; Saints and Angels came running to find Pope Bill pointing to a singe letter of a word on a parchment, repeating over and over: "There's an 'R'! Look! There's an 'R'! The word is 'celebrate', not 'celibate'!"

On being Irish:

Sundays in Lent are time-outs. The Irish would take a time-out on Good Friday if it fell on St. Patrick's Day.

"Being Irish he had an abiding sense of tragedy which sustained him through temporary periods of Joy." —William Butler Yeats

Bridget O'Malley goes to Father O'Grady in tears: "Ah Bridget, what can be so wrong as to upset you so?"

"Oh, Father, I've got terrible news, me husband died last night!"

"God save us," replies the priest. "Tell me, Bridget, did he make any last request?"

"That he did, Father. Mr. O'Malley asked me: "Bridget, for God's sake, put down that gun!"

A four-year-old, after going to bed one night, was having a nightmare. She awoke frightened, convinced that in the darkness all around her were these spooks and monsters. She felt desperately alone. And so she ran to her parents' bedroom to wake them. Her mother calmed her down and led her back to her own room, where she put on a light and reassured the child with these words: "Now you don't have to be afraid. You are not alone here. God is in the room with you." The child whimpered, "I know God's here, but I need someone in this room who has some skin!"

Woe! The first time I ever heard the word was on my father's ranch. It was the word the horse understood to mean to stop: Whoa! My dad had a special horse, he was a charismatic horse, a fundamentalist type, and the only words he would respond to were "Praise the Lord" and "Amen." So instead of "gitty up" you'd say "Praise the Lord," and instead of "whoa," you'd say Amen. One day a cowboy wanted to ride the horse. and my dad instructed him on the peculiarities of this particular steed. And so the cowpoke mounted the charismatic horse and said, "Gitty up," and nothing happened. Then he said "Praise the Lord," and off he rode, and the more he said, "Praise the Lord," the faster the horse galloped, until the edge of a cliff loomed up, and the cowboy yelled "Whoa," but the horse raced forward. At the last moment he remembered, and yelled "Amen" at the very brink, and the charismatic horse stopped. The cowboy took his Stetson off, wiped his forehead and prayed: "Praise the Lord."

Two factory workers, finishing their night shift went into a café nearby for breakfast. The waitress, who looked like she'd been there for thirty years approached her two customers with, "Well, what are you havin'?" One said: "Danish and coffee." The other guy said: "Bacon and eggs, please, and a kind word!" She shrugged while writing their orders, and left for the kitchen. When she returned she gave one guy the Danish and coffee and the other the bacon and eggs with: "Anything else?" The bacon and eggs guy asked: "No kind word?" The waitress on leaving their table paused and then replied: "I wouldn't eat those eggs if I were you!"

Repent —January 29, 1997

Here in his weekly church bulletin, Bill is speaking of being arrested and sent the Alameda County jail in Santa Rita, California, after being arrested for trespassing at Lawrence Livermore Laboratory, part of whose mission is development of nuclear weapons.

Fifty or so of us had landed in the Santa Rita bucket for trespassing onto Livermore Lab property, protesting nuclear bomb building. We were all crowded into one room to be booked, when a young deputy, quite excited, burst into the cellblock yelling: "Is there a priest in here?" Rather puzzled I put up my hand and pointed to my Roman collar; he had to be a Catholic school product from what he next said: "Father, you have to go to confession and repent!" I answered: "Confess and repent I agree, but not for this action, it's bomb builders who need to repent."

> And so my priesthood tends to be good news for those people with whom I stand, and the test of that authenticity is the grinding of teeth of those people I stand against.

Sometimes I feel like the little bird on a clouded wintry day lying in the middle of the road with its feet up in the air. A horseman rides up and looks down and inquires, "Little Bird, why are you lying the road with your feet up in the air?"

"As you can see, sir, the sky is about to fall and I'm here to hold it up."

And the horseman begins to laugh and wonders, "With those spindly little legs, how can you possibly succeed?"

The little bird says, "One does what one can."

Prayer

Bill both wrote prayers and wrote about prayer. Prayer for him was of course more than reciting common prayers. It could be quiet meditation, a moment of perceived presence of God. It could also be cry of anguish, as in "Out of the depths I cried out to you." Sometimes Bill's prayer was even an expression of frustration that God simply was not present to him.

When we are absolutely miserable, prayer is no longer a dry rote repetition. It becomes a living and vibrant cry for help. It becomes authentic. In pain we forget the "thees" and "thous" that separate us from God, and reach a new state of intimacy that comes from talking to God in our own way, saying what is in our heart. Such a prayer just could be more powerful than the way Jesus prayed when he began the "Our Father."

Suffering is a sign of our yearning for healing. The ultimate healing is being intimate with God. In this way suffering can be a way of being intimate with God.

The following prayer is the last one that Bill put into writing, dated December 1, 2003, a week before he died:

Dear God, or as each know you,
In our loneliness, comfort us,
in our sorrows, strengthen us,
In our frustrations, point out to us
that it is through suffering that we
are purified.

Show us that we are needed in our community.
We are needed by kindred souls who need to be listened to
and in our listening . . . you hear our cry for healing,
We each are so needed for the work of health giving.
Give us a deep faith in others,
in ourselves, and in You . . .
bright and firm hope which will ever increase in the journey
to You, who is the Journey. Dare we thank you,
God, for our pain, if it leads to your open embrace? Amen.

> I wear a collar that gives me the right to pray—it's more than a right, it's an absolute necessity and so let me pray:

God there is only one prayer, a prayer with one word, worthy of your hearing it is: To be free.
That sole quality that makes us human, the reflection of your glory. This masterpiece is called person, and to be a whole person is to be a part of society—to be excluded, then not to have a job, a house, to heal or get well is the making of a non-person—such social policy is damnable . . .

> God lead us from complexity to simplicity,
> From fear to trust,
> From being a crowd to community,
> from being unorganized to organized.
> God, bless our struggle to be free,
> Free from disease,
> Free for living and God, we bless you now and forever.
> Amen.

God of light, you reveal to us how the forces of darkness would blind us to your love for us . . . you will all your children to live in dignity and with respect, whatever is fit to being human; respect, giving the honor due to a person, simply because they are human.

God of Justice, when law fails, indeed disrespects our right to respect and denies our right to dignity, such law is a curse and deserves to be broken.

> There are many "Eucharists" celebrated other than the ritual prescribed by the Commission on Liturgy in the Vatican.

Women sitting around a coffee table do "Eucharist" unofficially because the regs say Tsk! Tsk! The doers of these Masses figure, to enter the grace world of sharing is more vitalizing than obeying a no-no that seems so unreasonable to them. They, we all, are on the road to Emmaus. If we do not let our eyes be opened and recognize him in the breaking of the bread, then indeed we are spiritually lost on life's road.

Jesus healed the Canaanite woman as well as her lunatic daughter. It's what we let divide us that makes all crazy. Jesus heals, frees us from that crazy-maker in us when we kneel at the Lord's feet and beg like the Canaanite woman, "Help Me."

Jesus' whole purpose was to call us out of our sleep, to make us aware that without God, there is no meaning to a world that is indeed absurd.
Without God, what's left but gabbing at whatever will remove that ache, that gnawing emptiness, that black hole in the center of our being.

Jesus claimed to be the God-Bread, the true soul food. The formula for health is contained in the Sermon on the Mount, the Lord's Prayer, in the parables. The Good News is that we can be healthy forever; the powerful sign and pledge is consuming the God Bread, where God becomes a part of us and we a part of God, and this is evidenced in how we support and serve one another.

A South African priest prays:
Silent Father; Silent Son; Silent Holy Spirit;
Silent One, I love you.
In the Silence of eyes, I see you;
in the silence of unspoken words, I hear you.
In the silence of sudden touch, I feel you.
In the silence of a flower's fragrance, I smell you.
In the silence of bread and wine, I taste you.
Sensual God, I love you! I love you in the silence,
Silent Father Silent Son, Silent Holy Spirit
Silent One—I love you. (Harry Alfred Wiggert)

Lord Jesus, victim of cruel and unusual punishment, our world is unfair. Our world holds: "Them's without the capital get the punishment."
Our world is insane; we execute the insane.
Our world is racist; we execute the minority.
Our world is stupid; we kill people to deter people from killing people.
Our world is hateful; we know the death penalty is a hate crime.
Our world is revengeful; we are fooled to believe peace comes through revenge.
Gentle Jesus, executed for our being unfair, insane, racist, stupid, hateful and revengeful: We pray:
Show us your world, a world that breaks the circle of violence.
Lord, crucified for our sins, lead us into your Love-life world. Amen.

Prayer at an Event for the Homeless, Malibu, California, 1996

God of the living, keep us alive,
all alive with the gifts your land provides;
Provident God, bless the providers;
the sowers, planters, harvesters, and the bakers of bread.
Providing God, let this food be the song of contradiction:
your bread, wasted by the rich;
denied to the poor, and wielded as if it were
a weapon by the powerful.
We trespass on the land with those whose rights
have been trespassed upon. Sharing your gifts with one another makes us one, as you did your friends,
Lord, on the night before the powerful broke your body for sharing your bread,
we pray that those who deny the hungry will never have to beg to eat. As your bread nurtures our bodies,
let your Spirit feed our hunger to be free,
to be one, to be alive.
Let it be the sign of your Presence;
let it be what bonds us as your sons and daughters.
We break bread, as you did with friends the night before you

gave your life that we may be free to live as you lived.
We give this bread to each other, nurturing one another.
We pray for the powerful who deny this bread-sharing that
they never become dependent on another to eat.
As your bread nurtures our bodies,
may your Spirit satisfy the hunger in our souls to be free,
to be loved, to be alive. Amen.

> Father all loving and all just, show me the suffering of the most miserable, so I will know my people's plight. Free me to pray for others, for you are present in every person. Help me to take responsibility for my own life, so, that I can be free at last.
> Grant me courage to serve others, for in service there is true life. Give me honesty and patience, so that I can work with other workers. Bring forth the song and celebration so that the Spirit will be alive among us, so that we will never tire of the struggle. Let us remember those who have died for justice, for they have given us life. Help us love even those who hate us, so, we can change the world. Amen.

This vacuum feeling is an opening
to our deepest mystery, to a sacred place,
where God can be experienced.
A place where we can reach out
from deep inside ourselves to take in the wonder
and strength and help that surrounds us.
This can keep us going for today,
keep us hoping for today . . . loving for today.

> Courage is believing that to lose life is to have it,
>   and the coward is fearing to die
>   and will grasp at anything to live.

Nature has created us with the capacity to know God,
to experience God, just as it has created us with the capacity
to know speech.
The experience of God (which is Grace)
or the possibility of experiencing God, is innate.

San Francisco Labor Breakfast, December 15, 1989

God of life whom we name Father, Son, Spirit,
we acknowledge our ownership of the raw ingredients of
our Trinitarian life forms: sex, religion and politics;
we praise you for these gifts.
These three powers of our soul are expressed in work: mind
work, art work, body work; meeting, organizing, acting;
when our work is not acknowledged we die a little,
when our work is exploited we die more,
When our work is denied, we die.
Coming together, praying together, living together is essential
to our being fully human.
The Trinity of evil—greed, abuse, betrayal—divides us,
diminishes us, destroys us. Whatever denigrates our labor is
our challenge to fight, to suffer crucifixion if need be.
God, we pray for the grace, the wisdom, the will, the energy
to work freely to be fully sexual, religious, and political.
Hear our prayer, God of life. Amen.

Instituto Banquet for Unions,
San Francisco Hilton, May 9, 2000

Justice be with you. Lord, make us instruments of your
justice.
Lord, inspire us at Instituto Laboral de la Raza to be a house
of refuge for workers from across our borders, whose backs
would be near broken by profiteers without conscience.
We work to protect who come to us for protection.
Lord, bless us both.
We work to guide workers whose bosses would misguide.
Lord, bless the guide and the guided.
We are the bridge for border crossers, seeking work here to
feed their families.
Lord, bless us all.
We are the sanctuary for workers in danger far from their
homes.
Lord, bless all in the sanctuary.
We are the lamp for workers without light.
Lord, you enlighten all from this meeting.
We are the safety net for workers pushed to fall into the

black hole of injustice.
Lord make us strong.
Keep our doors of welcome open to our day workers, who stand on street corners each morning, so vulnerable to vultures hovering for a killing.
Lord, make us instruments of your justice: we pray for all who are discriminated against because of race, color, religion, or sex, for those hounded for being profiled as unpatriotic. For those too weak to help themselves, for the jobless who search for work and there is no work.
We pray for ourselves who live in a merciless system perpetuating injustice; we pray for the wisdom and courage to change that system.
Lord you call us to union, for together, no force for greed can endure against our passion for justice.
Lord, we pray for the blessing of leadership on our servants; of the workers, Linda Chavez-Thompson; on Earl "Marty" Averette; on the Roofers and Waterproofers Local 40, and on our special guest, the Attorney General of California, Bill Lockyer.
Lord, make us all instruments of your justice. Amen.

> Praise is a way to say: "Thank you, Lord," regardless of the fight. Just to be grateful for surviving the last struggle you've been in is healthy.

Gratitude is not a reaction, it is a state of mind. A sense of well-being does not come from outside us. It comes from a sense that inside us we have the power to withstand whatever is outside us that threatens to destroy the equilibrium that makes the moment bearable.

To be grateful and to be thankful are not the same thing. It's easy to be polite and not mean it. Who hasn't been rubbed up against, or hit, and the rude person says, "Oh, excuse me" and you know they don't mean it. It's spiritual to be grateful, to do for another what has been done for us.

> Having a sense of gratitude can transform
>   an ordinary day into one of thanksgiving,
>   make a routine job a joyful one
>   and turn ordinary opportunities into blessings.

Anyone can complain, put down or find fault with what we have or don't have, but to love, value and appreciate what is ours is the challenge, indeed the invitation to be wholesome.

Blessing God is acknowledging God out of the turmoil, frustration, despair and failure of one's life—when all else fails, Bless God to survive!

Father Bill's Last Thanksgiving Dinner Prayer

Shared on his last Thanksgiving November 26, 2003:
We acknowledge no higher power than you, Lord, God, Allah. We give thanks day by day for your pushing us to show up where we are called. For the vision to see ourselves as we are . . . with no pretensions.

> We give thanks for being your living miracles, as we shun matters of trivial import, such as fundamentalist moralities, ethics, laws, customs, doctrines, etc. for the wisdom and courage to speak the truth to ourselves, to one another, to you the God of Abraham, to you the Allah of the Prophet, and to you Lord, Jesus.

We are not here to feed off this community, but indeed to feed this community with our service We are here to do our duty, that is to do whatever this day demands of us. Thank you Lord God on High, Almighty Power. Amen.

The 70th Wedding Anniversary of Maude and Anthony O'Donnell, Father Bill's parents, November 30, 1985

This prayer for his parents and family was part of the intercessions at a mass in celebration of the anniversary.

Intercessions:

Father Bill:
God, Father of us all, you will each of us to be of your kingdom, to serve one another in justice, love, and peace, therefore we make the following petitions:

Mary O'Donnell:
"That you accept Dad's and Mom's faithfulness to one another as a sign of their faithfulness to you . . . Let us pray to the Lord.

That their children, and their children's children accept the legacy handed down to them; which is do what is right and be right in what we do. . . . Let us pray to the Lord.

That Mother Mary Anthony and her daughters, the Little Sisters of the Poor, will continue to serve their resident guests as faithfully as Mary served her Son, the Word of God. Let us pray to the Lord.

That the workers and volunteers, so committed in their respect for these elders will continue to be patient and understanding. . . . Let us pray to the Lord.

That this day's blessings shower upon all relatives and friends of Maude and Anthony, that this celebration today deepen their love for one another, and may live forever. . . . Let us pray to the Lord.

That our own, ill of mind and body, through their crucifixion may experience healing and new life. . . . Let us pray to the Lord.

That our brothers Martin and Gene, our sister Betty,

Ed and Janie's Cathy, and all deceased members of the O'Donnell and Regan families live life to the full in Paradise . . .

Let us pray to the Lord.

Faith

Faith, for Bill, had nothing to do with the popular idea that it is "belief" in religious doctrines or narratives as if they were scientifically verifiable. For him, the words were closer to the word "trust," which is closer to the actual meaning of the New Testament Greek word usually translated as "believe." This is why he so frequently used the word "trust." Even if God did not seem present at a given time, a trust that he would be could sustain a person through the worst trials. This trust was a powerful antidote to fear and anxiety. Fear paralyzed, but that fear could be displaced by grace, which would grow out of trust. It was the ability of faith to displace fear that helped Bill take risks and face dangers that many of us would never have confronted.

He repeatedly criticized the popular notion that faith was merely a matter of the individual's relationship with God. He insisted that faith in God grew through relationships with others, because, as the gospels made clear, God dwelt in others and revealed Himself through others. This was in line with the gospel statement, "Whatever you do to the least of my bretheren, you do unto me." Faith that did not involve community and did not reveal itself through action was for Father Bill suspect, and could even be a form of narcissism.

However, if action deepens faith, faith in turn sustains action. It was a mutually reinforcing process, from inner to outer, outer to inner that strengthened and sustained. Or, as he put it: "Faith without action is day-dreaming. Action without faith is burn-out."

Everything bad that happens to us is a wake-up call.
God never allows anything to happen to us except that
it move us to acknowledge one simple faith-truth.
God is here.

The possible response to the "realities," the value of our humanness lies in not what we do, but in who we are. Our dignity, our worth, our value is given to us because each human is a child of God. Even Hitler. Even Osama Bin Laden. Moral decision-making depends on believing that. Where there is faith, there is truth. That's why the Word was born, why the Christ was murdered. God affirming His belief in our being God's inviolable child. Jesus promised if you believe strong enough, you can move even Mt. Diablo!

God talks to us in, by, and for church. We go to church more to share God than to find God. The church does its best work in the gutter. Only when church is humble, does its teaching become more believable. The church exists by mission, as fire exists by burning. No mission? No church . . . No church? No faith . . . No faith? . . . time to fear!

When I am in the present,
now, present myself to the Presence of God,
I may well experience the profound joy
offering myself as a present.
When Mary and Joseph presented Jesus
that day in the Temple,
their joy would have no end.

Who knows what Original Sin is,
except that we are all born blind spiritually.
God then gives us the grace to see ourselves,
others, and the world as God sees all.
The potential for this may come with baptism,
but this particular grace of spiritual sight may
come directly from God at any time in one's life.

God is real; God is close;
God is involved; God cares.
If we believe this to be true, then whatever challenge the world throws our way, we can handle it. Nothing can crush us. Even what's tough can make us stronger. No loss,

no death, no divorce, no punishment can, make us wimp out, but can actually stiffen us for future struggles.

The gospels used a metaphor for solidarity. Jesus has built his church on a rock in the person of Peter. This church was to be as solid as a rock. And whenever it got soft, wishy washy, worldly, and not faithful to its mission, then expect division, and a scattering.

Holding tight to the spirit of its founder is at the heart of the church's life. Whenever it behaves like the Pharisee, then expect cover-ups, secrecy, hypocrisy, and being a scandal to the world. It deserves the shame it brings down on top of its hard head.

> "Accept surprises that upset your plans,
> shatter your dreams, give a completely
> different turn to your day, and who knows
> —to your life. It is not chance.
> Leave the Father free to weave
> the pattern of your days."

We don't know tomorrow's agenda. Just to be in the now, and not to pretend. They say if you want to make God laugh, tell God what your plans are for tomorrow. Being cool, or living in holy carelessness, living the present, keeps you alive with purpose.

> Yesterday is gone, but the consequences
> of my negative behavior may have to be made up for,
> if it had hurt someone. That's enough to make
> the present pregnant. Tomorrow is unreal
> until it gets here. It belongs to God anyway
> and when I let that be, tomorrow becomes mine.

To see, to possess intimacy with God is the soul's passion. Yet, no soul pursues more passionately than God does.

Jesus talked about how absolutely committed God is to us, absolutely faithful; God is incapable of not loving each of us; we can trust God; God will never betray us.

> The mystery of God-with-me and
> I-with-God depends wholly on God
> to the extent there is no "I" without God.
> When I am with God, then I am who and what I am.

> When I am against God, I am struggling to destroy
> who and what God creates and saves me to be.
> This struggle is futile; I cannot rid myself of
> God's presence in my being and life.
> To persist in it is madness and hell.

I've heard that accepting completely the fact that we are going to die helps us to be fully alive; when we do, fear and stress strangely leave us; we begin to drink in the beauty around us; to begin to listen to the music our souls long for, read the books that most delight us, enjoy the wonders of nature, spend time with those we love, in a word we can chill out in ease.

> 'Tis imperative to recognize the difference between possession and use.
> The beauty and wonder of the environment, of art, of architecture around us need not be possessed to be enjoyed. It even comes as a shock that our obsession to possess interferes with our ability to enjoy.
> Imagine owning Yosemite. How could you enjoy it with hordes of tourists clamoring to get in? It's the difference between lust, the urge to possess, and love, the need to share. Anyway, ownership is relative, never absolute, depending on the common good.
> Possession may serve to quench one's thirst for security and control, but at the same time it tends to warp, even destroy, our more basic need to enjoy beauty wherever we find it.

Freedom, the quality that makes us human, above the animal, like the angels, depends on being our authentic selves, conscious of how deeply connected we are to one another; passionate about serving primarily the unable. In a word, a humble person is the most joyful, the kindest, the least phony. The humble attracts like a magnet. The proud repels like a bad smell.

> Faith without action is day-dreaming.
>   Action without faith is burn-out.

> Faith begins this experiencing the kingdom.
> Repentance, or radical change blows the tubes, clarifies, our essence, opens up the heart to love as Jesus loves.

> What God reveals to us is the gift to us.
> Our believing is our gift to God.

I think the salvation of the world depends on people coming together. Faith is a four-pronged star; the center represents God. Being a star, it's a light in a very dark world. The first prong stands for prayer, where we listen to God speak to our hearts; the second prong represents the grace of giving, which means we share who we are and what we have; the third prong is unconditional love with God and members of the community; the forth prong of the star represents community, where democracy is to be practiced in the community and outside the community. When people organize to form these kinds of community, no force on earth can destroy them. On the promise of Jesus that "I will be with you until the end of the earth."

> God does not exist to approve or not approve of my behavior; the gospel is saying that you and I exist because God wants us to. And the more faithful I am to God, the more alive I am; the less faithful to God the more dead I am.

Where there is faith, there is truth.

The root meaning of disciple is one who is a learner; more than a student who completes courses; it means one who continually imbibes the mystery of Jesus, whose understanding never ceases to deepen, and who continually applies this growing knowledge in creating a way of life that more and more approximates the way Jesus thought, spoke and acted.

> The greatest ying-yang with Jesus was faith
> as the antidote to fear, not good versus bad,
> nor the just against the unjust;
> not truth over falsehood, not even love as the
> response to hate. Fear not; have faith.

When Jesus invited people to follow him, he meant that they be like him, To take command of their lives and live what they believe and believe what they live. The servant leader first becomes one with God. And, no longer able to play God, but be like God, then becomes one with those they serve. Call it atonement, as in at-one-mended.

Joy comes not from the satisfaction of an appetite.
Not to be confused with pleasure.
Too often the pursuit of pleasure is the substitute for the pursuit of joy.
Pleasure comes from getting; joy comes from letting go.
With pleasure there's always a price.
With joy there's always a gain.
Without faith a person is capable only of pleasure.
To know joy, it takes faith.
Pleasure comes from a binding of some kind.
Joys come from being free.
Pleasure comes from without; joy, from within.
Joy is God-centered; pleasure, creature-centered.
Joys comes from grace; pleasure from graciousness.

Crocheted in a picture frame, hanging on a wall of a priest's room, I remember as a kid, reading: "Joy is the infallible sign of the presence of God."

When anxiety, worry and fear, when anger, resentment, and rage invade my heart, any one of these spells a threat to the end of faith. The opposite is equally true. The beginning of true faith can make these downers, from anxiety to rage, poof away. These negatives can choke out the breath of faith, if I let them. To let these soul pollutants fester is to wallow in self-pity. Faith mirrors God's beauty and truth, and like life, is a many splendored thing.

My faith in the Gospel dictates that, spiritually, racism is inconceivably inhuman, and makes the offender ugly. Racism is the primary evil in the U.S., along with militarism and consumerism.

By racism I mean to include all prejudice and negative discrimination of any kind against not only race, but ethnically different persons. A great blessedness would descend on our world if all suffered from the incurable disease of color blindness.

In John's first letter; whoever is a child of God conquers the world, i.e., ones who separate out from the rat race. The vehicle is faith, starting with what you don't believe in, and that is any human institution claiming to solve all human problems, as once the scientific world promised, until it brought the world the H-Bomb.

Believing in what counters the violence of the world
   is to begin conquering the world.
      Faith that God is Love is a beginning.

Faith that every human being is inviolate,
   from the fetus to the elderly, that all violence,
      be it attitudinal, mental, verbal,
         or physical is unconscionable.

"Ephphatha,"
"BE OPENED," cries Jesus to the deaf man who had a speech impediment. To be opened to any person who speaks from the heart is to be open to God speaking through that person, even if that person is a non-believer. Who has not their truth to be spoken. To be faithful to myself, to you, and to God, I owe you to listen to you.

Life is inviolable: to allow the tiniest crack in this understanding of life, is to open the flood gates to violence from snuffing one fetus to a wholesale nuclear holocaust. Rationalize one killing and why not a million. Death is natural. To cause a death violates the fundamental right to life.

Be Not Afraid—June 27, 1993

"Do not be afraid." Three times, Jesus urges his friends: "Do not be afraid." I was afraid last week even though I really enjoyed Washington, D.C. I went there to celebrate a Jesuit friend becoming a priest.

But, wouldn't you know! As soon as I deplaned, my greeters, Catholic Workers in D.C., said, "We're doing a civil disobedience action at the White House, calling for a Comprehensive Nuclear Test Ban: No testing, even underground.

The White House has a 10-foot metal-spear fence in the front. Three people were designated to lock themselves to the fence with bicycle locks and bungie cords. We helped one man, who'd been fasting for 33 days, to climb over the fence, and sit down at the base, and we slipped the bicycle lock around his neck. Another man did the same except he was on the outside of the fence. We were scared and clumsy about getting the locks fastened. The Secret Service moved so fast that we didn't get the third person locked to the fence.

The adrenaline was rushing in everybody—in ourselves, tourists observing all this—even the Secret Service—one young one drew his .45 and leveled it at the protester locked inside the fence and yelled: "Get up or I'll blow your head off!" "He can't! His neck is locked to the fence!" I said. Others yelled similar things. The sergeant in charge analyzed the scene and saw no chance of violence, waved off the Secret Service with a stand- slack-off, gesture.

The point of this little story—fear. It gripped everybody. Fear can be paralyzing—freezing, it stuns. Fear can make us forget, furious, frustrated. Fear can make us angry, fear can trigger rage, can't walk around in rage more than 10 seconds, so what do we do? Suppress it, or repress it. And to KEEP IT OUT OF SIGHT we use drugs, alcohol, and ego!

Fears blocks me from doing God's will, from following Jesus, even to the Cross.

"Do not be afraid," Jesus assures his friends. If I'm afraid, maybe I am not a friend of Jesus, maybe I'm not close enough to God. Fear fails Faith—Fear blocks vision, blinds my view of God's world.

It's not courage that it takes to do justice and make peace . . . . It's faith—if my faith is strong enough I can do anything . . . Jesus promised. But if I have more fear than faith, I can do nothing!

It's Evil that scares me. Evil in its all-pervasive million forms is what makes me behave not at all like God made me to behave. I have to name it, define it, unmask it, detoxify it, destroy, or contain it. Evil never surrenders without a fight.

"Do not be afraid of anything." Love the person who would betray you, use you, injure you . . . would kill you. After all . . . that person is us.

Hope

Having been engaged in union, peace, and civil rights struggles for decades, Bill took the long view, and like many movement veterans realized that victories were not won overnight, and that one had to have a broad historical sense of social change. This required hope that could answer the question "How long?" with "As long as it takes." Father Bill's ultimate example for hope was the fact that the first followers of Jesus seemed completely crushed when he was crucified, yet out of this brutal execution arose a faith that gives hope to individuals and movements throughout the world.

Understand that hope is not born out of certainty. You don't hope the sun will set this evening . . . it will! Hope begins and ends in what stirs our hearts, where we place our trust, how we conduct our lives. There's no logic to hope, no rationality. Hope is born from the longing for something better—a craving, a die-for pounding need for the improbable.

> The problems we see are right in front of us.
> Hope is visualizing problems into solutions.

>> God never has given up on a world hell-bent toward the precipice of destruction by myopic architects with technological genius.

>> God's Word lives.

One Rider's Report—October 12, 2003

Logging over 20,000 miles, over 900 Freedom Riders for Immigrant Rights, in 18 buses, speaking 50 different languages, originating from 10 different cities, rally at 103 cities en route to lobby Congress, to conclude this twelve-day trek across America, at Liberty's Statue, sang this message wherever we arrived: "We all may have come to these shores in different boats, but we are all in the same boat now!" In our mission we preached lies in the solution.

Workable and Just Policies that Strengthen America and Live Up to Our Ideals: 1) Reward labor by granting legal status to hardworking, taxpaying, law-abiding immigrants already established in the United States. 2) Renew our democracy by clearing the path to citizenship and full political participation for our newest Americans. 3) Restore labor protections so that all workers, including immigrant workers, have fair treatment on the job. 4) Reunite families in a timely fashion by streamlining our outdated immigration policies; and 5) Respect the civil rights and civil liberties of all so that immigrants are treated equally under the law; so that the federal government remains subject to checks and balances, and civil rights laws are meaningfully enforced.

This historic demonstration, originated from unions such as the hotel and restaurant workers local, from laborers union locals, and UNITE, the needle and textile locals, garment workers, convinced the AFL-CIO leadership to reverse its longstanding opposition to immigration and to sponsor this million-dollar Immigrant Worker Freedom Ride journey across America.

The purpose was to raise the consciousness of the public to this neo-slavery of people desperate enough to leave their homes, to come here crossing our borders or to come to our shores, to seek a decent life through always being willing to accept the kind of work abhorrent to our citizens. Our outdated system forces many immigrant families to be separated from loved ones for years, even decades. Many simply won't endure the separation from their families and instead risk their lives and their future by living here without legal status. We should reward the hard work of those with roots in our communities and who have a track record of good behavior by putting these workers and their families on the road to citizenship. Moses took 40 years to reach the Promised Land. This struggle? As long as it takes. —The OD

The weapon to counter terrorism is Hope.
And by Hope I don't mean Optimism.
Optimism is some kind of in-vain belief
that things will turn out the way I would like.

Hope comes when you're thoroughly convinced
something is moral, ethical and right.
Hope makes you fight for it regardless of the consequences.

On the other hand, optimism, wishing things
to be like they should, can be a doorway
into disappointment; then down stairs to pessimism,
finally to crash into the basement of despair.
The other side of optimism is depression.

Hope is where there's no logic or reason,
independent of provable facts.
Hope gets powerful when it releases human energies
that generate a passionate longing for something better.
It's like romance, illogical, rather insane,
but a nuclear explosion of passion to conceive,
birth, and nurture those infant twins, justice and freedom.
Then peace flows like a river.

Hope transfigures. No matter how hard the struggle,
you shall overcome, because God promised you
the strength to endure to the last.

The world could not tolerate his wisdom and thought.
It obliterated it on Golgotha's dump heap.
Instead, it unleashed a spirit that refuses to be
imprisoned inside a mortal body or be
restricted by time and clime.

It's why the Word took on skin and was born Jesus. This Jesus showed us how to live and promised he'd never abandon us. How he did that, is how we celebrate Pentecost. Jesus promised us an Advocate, that the very Spirit of God would live in every heart to inspire, to empower any person to believe as Jesus believed, never to give up hope, and to love no less than Jesus loves.

Bill and Cesar Chavez, leader of the United Farm Workers (UFW), in 1974. When Bill learned about the substandard wages and living conditions of farm workers in California and across the nation, he joined their protest marches and spoke of their plight and their right to unionize. Chavez stayed at the Saint Joseph the Worker "safe house" when he was in the San Francisco Bay Area.

Sister Betty O'Donnell, SNJM, Bill's sister and UFW organizer, Salinas, California. When Sister Betty returned from work in Peru and asked Bill where the action was, he replied "UFW." She went into the fields and organized the workers.

Bill and friends protest nuclear weapons research at the Lawrence Lab, Livermore, California, in 1982. Bill's motto: "Show up, make a friend, have fun." At one Livermore protest a policeman seized Bill and broke his arm.

In commemoration of Good Friday and in protest of nuclear weapons, a vigil is held at the gates of the Lawrence Livermore Lab. Here Bill spoke out against war and for peace.

Arrest at Oakland, California, dockworkers' protest.

Protest in support of an airline mechanics strike.

Bill's acting career: He played an army chaplain praying for his men in Martin Sheen's 1989 antiwar film, *Nightbreaker.*

Bill and friends lead a vigil at the School of the Americas/WHISC in memory of the six Jesuit priests, their housekeeper, and her fifteen-year-old daughter murdered in El Salvador, and thousands of others murdered by the military in Central America. Left to right: Dr. Davida Coady, activist in international health care and in substance-abuse treatment; actor Martin Sheen; a friend; Bill, and author/peace activist Father John Dear.

Bill speaks out in support of field workers in El Salvador.

Another arrest.

Bill and friends in Korea. When Bishop John Cummins of the Diocese of Oakland was talking to a priest while visiting Korea, the cleric said, "Oh, yes, your Father Bill O'Donnell was here last week."

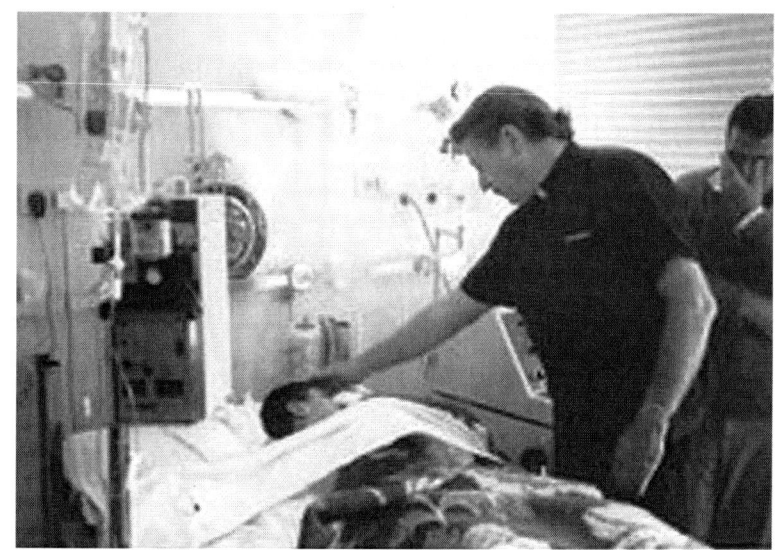

On a peace mission to Palestine, Bill comforts a wounded child.

Bill gleefully joins in a passing protest march in London.

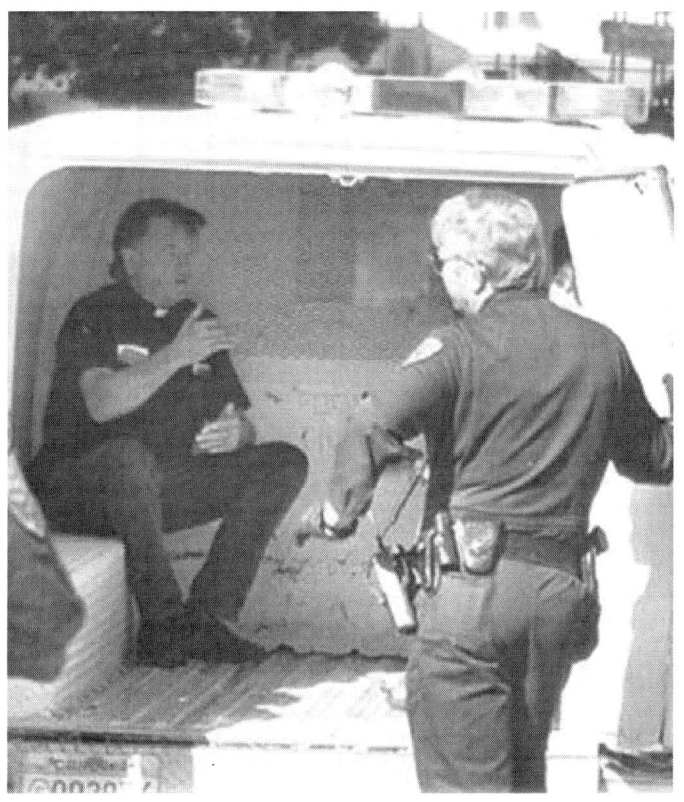

Bill explains the Constitutional right to protest to an arresting officer.

Bill and Sister Helen Prejean, CSJ, author of *Dead Man Walking*, in November 2003 at the SOA/WHISC vigil at Fort Benning, Georgia, two weeks before his death on December 8, 2003.

Bill holding a cross of remembrance with the name of one of the victims of murder by the military in El Salvador.

Left: Bill, Mary, and Jim O'Donnell during a prison visit in Spring 2003. No visitor could wear tan or green clothing, and each had to be screened before being allowed into the large room where Bill and his fellow prisoners held their visits.
Right: Bill says good-bye to a fellow prisoner. Bill started a Bible-study group while inside and counseled many of the men, and when requested by inmates would write to wives and families.

Bill, Mary O'Donnell, Dolores Huerta, and friends at the U.S. Federal Penitentiary in Atwater, California, in September 2002. Fearing that the group had assembled to attempt to free Bill, prison authorities ordered a lockdown of the entire facility.

After Mass at St. Joseph the Worker Church in April 2003, after his release from prison.

Diocese of Oakland
2900 LAKESHORE AVENUE
OAKLAND, CALIFORNIA 94610

May 31, 1972

Reverend William J. O'Donnell
Sacred Heart Church
4025 Grove St.
Oakland, CA 94609

Reverend and dear Father:

Confirming our conversation of Monday, May 22, I am herewith officially notifying you

1. not to use as elements of the sacrifice of the Mass anything but valid and traditional material;

2. not to use the Mass as a means of propaganda for any political cause, however valid and good the cause may be;

3. not to celebrate Mass outdoors and publicly without my permission.

If you violate this precept, it may lead to the suspension of your faculties in the Diocese of Oakland. I am not happy in imposing any such penalty and I hope that you will cooperate. I am in sympathy with your motives and with what you are trying to do. I do not forbid you to be concerned about the poor and their problems.

I am sincerely hopeful that we will understand each other.

Cordially yours,

Most Reverend Floyd L. Begin
Bishop of Oakland

flb:jvb

Ans'd June 13
Dear B. This is to acknowledge receipt of your letter of 5/31 in which this gave official written notification of 5/22. However this same oral instructions & directions of 5/22

A Memorial Resolution

By the Honorable Loni Hancock
14th Assembly District, Relative to memorializing

FATHER WILLIAM J. O'DONNELL

WHEREAS, The passing of a great and inspirational religious leader, Father William J. "Bill" O'Donnell, who was well known for his integrity, compassion, and deep concern for others, has brought great sadness and a deep sense of loss to the people of California; and

WHEREAS, Father Bill O'Donnell, a giant in the world of peace and social justice activism, passed away in Berkeley on December 8, 2003, at the age of 73; and

WHEREAS, Father O'Donnell was one of identical twins born in Livermore on January 2, 1930, and raised on a nearby farm; and he had six brothers and sisters, including Mary O'Donnell, an alcohol and drug recovery counselor whom he often described as "my best friend"; and

WHEREAS, Father O'Donnell entered St. Patrick's Seminary in Menlo Park in 1950 and was ordained six years later; and

WHEREAS, Father Bill resided at St. Joseph the Worker Catholic Church in Berkeley as Pastor and as Associate Pastor for the past 30 years; and

WHEREAS, He, a close friend of Caesar Chavez, worked with the United Farm Workers, Board Treasurer of San Carlos Foundation, Options Program, School of the Americas Watch, Labor Priest to the AFL/CIO, SEIU, Teamsters, and the Labor Counsel; and

WHEREAS, An outstanding contributor to society and a noble emissary for his state, Father Bill O'Donnell's life bore eloquent testimony to a brilliant career of public and religious service exemplified by the finest moral and civic leadership; and **WHEREAS,** He was preceded in death by his parents, Anthony and Maude O'Donnell and his siblings Martin, Eugene, and Betty Anne O'Donnell (Sr. Anthony Edward SNJM); and

WHEREAS, His memory will be cherished by his siblings Edward, Mary, and James; and his nieces and nephews, Jane, Steve, David, Matthew, Carol, Jeannie, Sean, Kevin, CeCe, Joe, Chrissy, Diane, and Shannon O'Donnell; now, therefore, be it

RESOLVED BY ASSEMBLY MEMBER LONI HANCOCK, That she joins the friends and family of Father William J. "Bill" O'Donnell in celebrating and revering the accomplishments and legacy of a distinguished and caring individual who lived life to the fullest, whose generosity was extended to everyone without hesitation or expectation of reward, and whose spirit will live forever in the hearts and memories of all of his loved ones.

Members Resolution No. 93

Dated this 11th day of December, 2003

UNITED STATES DISTRICT COURT
MIDDLE DISTRICT OF GEORGIA
PROBATION OFFICE

ROBERT R. LONG
SUPERVISING PROBATION OFFICER

U. S. POST OFFICE AND COURTHOUSE, RM 304
120 12TH STREET
COLUMBUS, GEORGIA 31901-2423

REPLY TO:
POST OFFICE BOX 990
COLUMBUS, GEORGIA 31902-0990

PHONE (706) 649-7818
FAX (706) 649-7825

August 21, 2002

William J. O'Donnell
1640 Addison Street
Berkeley, CA 94703

Dear Mr. O'Donnell:

This is to advise you that we have received notification from the Bureau of Prisons of the location designated for you to begin service of your sentence.

For service of this sentence, you are instructed to report to the USP Atwater, located at P.O. Box 019000, #1 Federal Way, Atwater, CA 95301, telephone: 209/386-4615, no later than 12:00 noon, on September 10, 2002.

Please give me a call upon receipt of this letter. My office telephone number is 706-649-7818.

Sincerely,

Wendy S. Howard

Wendy S. Howard
U. S. Probation Officer

WSH/pae

Enclosure

NEWS FROM . . .

Congresswoman Nancy Pelosi

2457 Rayburn Building, Washington, D.C. 20515   202-225-4965

July 2, 2002

House Democratic Whip Nancy Pelosi (D-CA) issued the following statement today at a press conference held by School of the Americas Watch West.

"Although Congressional business prevents me from being with you in person today, I appreciate the opportunity to receive this Declaration of Protest from Fr. Louis Vitale, Fr. William O'Donnell, and Leone Reinbold.

"Fathers Vitale and O'Donnell share a long history of activism for peace, justice and human rights, and have worked tirelessly on behalf of the most vulnerable members of society. I thank them for their important contributions to the San Francisco Bay Area and applaud their willingness to stand up for what is right.

"In 1999, the U.S. Congress voted to close the School of the Americas (SOA), which has educated some of the most horrible violators of human rights in this hemisphere. Last year, the Pentagon changed its name to the Western Hemisphere Institute for Security Cooperation (WHISC), but did little to address the fundamental issues raised by Congress about the school's training methods, its lack of oversight, and its record of graduating human rights abusers.

"I am proud to cosponsor H.R. 1810 that would repeal the authority of the Department of Defense to operate WHISC - effectively closing it. This legislation would also establish a joint congressional task force to evaluate what kind of education and training is appropriate to provide for military personnel of Latin American nations, particularly with respect to the observance of human rights.

"Human rights abuses by military personnel in Latin America are not, unfortunately, a thing of the past. We must not condone any of the atrocities that have been performed by people who are graduates of the School of the Americas, and I will continue to work with all of you to close this institution."

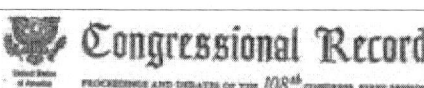

Congressional Record

PROCEEDINGS AND DEBATES OF THE 108th CONGRESS, FIRST SESSION

House of Representatives

HONORING FATHER BILL O'DONNELL

HON. BARBARA LEE
OF CALIFORNIA
IN THE HOUSE OF REPRESENTATIVES
Sunday, December 14, 2003

MS. LEE - Mr. Speaker, I rise today to honor a wonderful man and dedicated activist, Father Bill O'Donnell. Father O'Donnell died of a heart attack while at his desk writing a homily at St. Joseph's the Worker Catholic Church in Berkeley. The longtime priest known as the 'saint of Berkeley' died December 8 at age 73.

Bill O'Donnell was born in 1930 to a large Irish family who were farmers in Livermore, and attended St. Michael's church and school there. He told friends that his mother, Maude Regan O'Donnell, was the "one who inspired me." After graduation from St. Joseph's College in Menlo Park, he went to St. Patrick's Seminary there and graduated in June 1956. He was ordained in St. Mary's Cathedral in San Francisco, when Oakland was part of the San Francisco Diocese.

Father O'Donnell's first parish was St. Jarlath's in Oakland's Dimond district where he was assistant pastor from 1956 to 1963. From there, O'Donnell was sent to Corpus Christi Church in Piedmont from 1963-1965; St. Joseph's in Alameda, 1965-1966; St. Joachim, Hayward, 1966-1969; and Sacred Heart, Oakland, 1969-1973.

He once told a reporter he was "kicked out" of three parishes before finding his rightful home. That was his assignment in 1973 to St. Joseph's, which at the time was known as St. Joseph's the Workman. As assistant pastor, O'Donnell was instrumental in "de-gendering" the name to St. Joseph the Worker, to honor the work of women as well as men.

He was pastor there through August 1995 and chose to become associate pastor to allow more time for his activism. Rev. George Crespin, the present pastor, and O'Donnell were fast friends, as was recently retired Bishop John Cummins, who was always loyal to O'Donnell.

Many of his legions of friends regarded O'Donnell as the "saint of Berkeley" for his almost 250 arrests at protests, which included marching with union organizer Cesar Chavez. Most recently at Fort Benning, Ga., O'Donnell and 10,000 other protesters tried to shut down the controversial School of the Americas, which they say teaches terrorist tactics on behalf of dictators.

O'Donnell also repeatedly protested at Lawrence Livermore Laboratory, for which he once spent a week in Santa Rita County jail. During another protest, his arm was broken by a police officer.

While O'Donnell wasn't always associated with activism, the seeds were there waiting for something to bring them to life, he once said. At first he challenged the church itself but found his real life mission was with the labor, civil rights and peace movements.

Finally, as we honor Father O'Donnell today, I want to thank him for being an exemplary role model, spiritual leader, and hero. I take great pride in joining Bill's family, friends and colleagues to recognize and salute this man who spent his life standing up for causes when others looked the other way.

TEAMSTERS' JOINT COUNCIL NO. 7

AFFILIATED WITH THE INTERNATIONAL BROTHERHOOD OF TEAMSTERS

Serving the greater San Francisco Bay Area

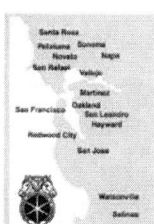

November 12, 2008

Ms. Mary O'Donnell
4 Commodore Dr. D-221
Emeryville, CA 94608

Dear Mary:

I look forward to the book. It will say a lot.

Father Bill was so exceptional. He wasn't your run-of-the-mill everyday Catholic priest. When he delivered the message, it wasn't just by word, more often by action.

He fought for the Lord and Catholicism but he also fought for workers, the poor, the down trodden and the addicted.

And it was never about him, it was never about ego…probably the most unassuming man since Jesus Christ.

Father Bill was my priest, my comrade and friend. He was also a mentor. He led by example.

Sincerely,

Chuck Mack
President

CM/jbo.ibc856

Father Bill saying mass at the Concord Naval Weapons Station, "asking Marines to join us." He wrote: "Later that A.M., in order to stop me advancing onto the base, the major on the right threw me down onto the tracks and arrested me!"

Father Louie Vitale, Franciscan priest and cofounder of Pace e Bene, a nonviolence organization; Delores Huerta, UFW cofounder and former UFW vice-president; Eloy Martinez, a UFW supporter and friend of Bill, and Fred Chavez.

Love

Father Bill's sermons and bulletins on love would themselves make up an entire volume. He realized that love was probably the most difficult religious task of all because it is extremely difficult to give unconditional love. For most of us, he thought, it required more effort than any other aspect of religious commitment.

~~~~~~~~~~~~~~~~~~

Love it is that makes whole these warring quarters within us. Love helps balance us as we walk life's tight rope, prevents us from falling into the pit of wants.

Love is our will, our heart choosing, preferring what or who is best for us; romantic love speaks more to what we want; but sometimes only to what we need. It's an in-betweener.

Jesus proposes:
Love God all the way, with all your heart, soul, and mind.
    This loving includes loving self all the way,
        no less including any other person loving all the way,
        as Frank Sinatra used to croon. "All" in Jesus' wording
        could be the crucial word in this commandment.
                Love means all or nothing.
Lovers may insist: take all of me, the good, bad, and ugly.
Jesus is saying we need to accept ourselves
    and the other unconditionally.

Did you know there are some things that even God can't do? For example God could not possibly say: "You must love the Lord your

God with all your heart, with all your soul, and with all your mind . . . and your neighbor as yourself," unless first God loved you and me with his total being unconditionally. When you think about it!

The Transfiguration experience is the sense of "never being the same again." Falling in love can do it. A near-death experience—anything. But don't try LSD. That's hallucinating and a fake. Have a real trip with God to God.

> A command to love a contradiction?
> To obey the demands of love is as vital as breathing.
> Who would not want to obey if it means a fuller life,
> if it means experiencing the joy of integrity,
> and wholeness.

> The original meaning of obey is to listen,
> not just hear, but intensely listen by meditating;
> it's when conscience will speak,
> and you will crave to obey its call to love.

> Alone time, where only the two of you walk and rest together.

Experiencing this in life gets us to know God in suffering, and in dying, when we get to see God face-to-face in resurrection. It's how Jesus did it.

> What constitutes a person is the ability to love . . . if not corrupted.

> Real humility is a process of being everything
> you can possibly be and helping everybody else
> to be their best, too.
> The primary and ultimate vocation is to be as human
> as possible; to struggle to become what God
> passionately wants us to be, i.e., free to love.
> Like God

Personable is how we describe God. And so our relationship can be intensely intimate because we too are persons who can love. See how we connect?

> To love a person is to have died to the need for that person
> to be something for you . . . and to be utterly alone.

God sees you and me as we actually are. God can't help but love us, for God is love. Because God sees us and the three persons of the Trinity in his aloneness, God knows us.

We must never cease to be aware of this quest to love; for that were we born, for that we would die.

Love springs from being aware, seeing.

It is only inasmuch as we see someone as he or she really is here and now—and not as they are in our memory or in our desire or in our imagination or projection—that we can truly love them.

Christmas is the Feast of Love,
challenge to the hearts, food for the mind,
life sounds to hear.
Christmas is peace for our troubles;
forgiveness of our guilt;
Christmas is God's coming for our loneliness.
God's light for our sharing and caring,
hearing the good news proclaimed by the angels,
the anticipation of the prophets,
that all is well when left to God.

The Gospel of Love indicates that consuming does not substitute for love. It's the distraction of distractions. War is another substitute . . . sex, religion, politics, anything can sub for love.

Jealous?
Afraid to lose your love?
Give it away.
Rather than possess, dispossess.
It begins the discovery of your own power to love self. Formidable. Envious?
Let it lead you to what you need more than somebody else's thing, the discovery of your own soul.
That is the most precious of all possessions.

Jesus seems to encourage us to be open to the Blessing that is always present, sometimes hidden, sometimes disguised. It takes waiting, but believe it's worth waiting for. All life is believing.

Jealousy and Envy keep life at bay, at a safe distance, and yet they do invite their carriers to enter more deeply the cavern of their hearts, where love that resides there can be reclaimed. "J" & "E" can be a blessing because they point to areas of life beyond reason into the very mystery of soul, indeed an exciting adventure.

Eavan Boland, Ireland's preeminent female poet, writes of a couple in 1847, during the Famine, who decide to leave the Workhouse for the Poor and return home. His wife, too weak to walk, is carried by her husband on his back. A true story. "In the morning they were both found dead of cold, of hunger, of the toxins of a whole history. But her feet were held against his breast bone. The last heat of his flesh was his last gift to her" and his first gift to her was his promise to love her . . . All the way.

Needs and wants sometimes are but the two sides of the same coin. A common mantra on a labor picket line might be: "no justice, no peace." It's saying, we need justice and want peace. In truth commissions established in nations after their civil wars, its preface reads: "There will be no peace without justice; no justice without truth; no truth without full accountability." When these wants and needs are satisfied, then forgiveness may flow, the ultimate act of genuine love.

Peace

Dedicated to nonviolence, Bill was long deeply engaged in the peace movement, both in protests against war and the military establishment, and through his sermons and bulletins. He participated in peace delegations to North Korea and Palestine. This aversion to violence extended to his opposition to capital punishment. He was a prominent figure in vigils at the San Quentin penitentiary whenever an execution was planned and carried out there. He constantly preached the lessons of nonviolence, especially the precept that peace was both personal and political, knowing that personal rage can easily be projected into political violence.

Pax . . . Paz . . . Pace . . . Peace

Peace is as peace does.
And what's that?
It's what you actually experience
as a feeling of harmony within,
a harmony in relationships.

Internally peace connotes a "freedom from disquieting or oppressive thoughts or emotions. It brings a sense of relaxation, "away from it all."

A major addition here is that genuine peace springs from genuine charity. This implies including consciously one's neighbor with the love of God. This suggests peace is pro-active, more than a quietude, but indeed a work of justice as in the slogan. "No justice, no peace."

So peace has to be made; not automatic like the sunrise. It implies change, indeed conflict. Gospel peace can be achieved through nonviolent direct action. No pain, no gain!

The premier community organizer, Saul Alinsky, found that peace is the "essence of community"—in contradistinction to institution. The former is the assembly of people, democratically organized, choosing to achieve an agreed-upon goal of justice.

> Jesus recognizes that we must prize conflict,
> engage in it up to but always short of violence.
> Conflict sharpens, refines, and purifies our persons.
> Conflict teaches one the consequence of violence,
> which can never be an option to what humanizes,
> cultivates, and civilizes. Conflict is the womb
> from which is born truth, justice, and freedom.
> Then only can love and life that inevitably follow happen.
> Reconciliation above conflict is a great temptation;
> as is preferring peace above justice;
> tranquility above truth, and security above freedom.

Corporate America's like one giant casino where bleary-eyed managers gamble, enthralled and mesmerized by the entertainment, games, and information, and risk all that is vital, alive, and human in our world on the chance that the big payoff will come, and Technology will finally solve all of our problems. Technology will make us rich, will bring peace and inner harmony. From such a drunk, organizing is the worker's recovery program. Our culture puts down the importance of friendships, putting in its place things like "quality time," which is technology's double speak substitute for real intimacy and connection. The television has become the family hearth. Computers and videos, the family mentors. Fast food the family meal.

Peace is when there are two people in a room, each in opposite corners; one holds a loaf of bread; the other is without. The one with can't go to sleep; if he does, the other will cross the room, kill him, and take the loaf. Wisely, the one with tears the loaf in half and gives the other a half, and they live happily ever after.

> I suspect that there are more genuine peacemakers in our world than there are soldiers.

"Peace is people talking together with a heart in between them." (Bobby, age 8)

The world outside the U.S. calls our world a wannabe empire, or as we prefer, an "empire in denial." The history of empires is one of people domination and market expansion at the point of the gun. The rich need empires, or they lose their power. The U.S. is hell-bent to control the world.

Pope John Paul saw our world in the U.S. as a death culture, whenever death is sanctioned to wage war, or the death penalty for murder, or abortion for economics, then it's worldly behavior. The world is described as that which produces.

Many multinational companies are larger and wealthier than most nations. Their boards of directors decide where your kids are going to die defending the corporations' right to invade and exploit native resources and populations.

> Humility urges me to own my part in the rage
> and murder of my neighbor's madness.
> Where have I failed to be my brother/sister's keeper?
> When I fail, I become a target/we all become
> a target for one another.
> When all communities take on responsibilities
> for one another then will hostile swords be beaten
> into plowshares.
> If I treat my neighbor's pain and grief as not mine,
> I'm making sure that their suffering will curdle
> into retaliation.
> Instead of being sucked into a war of retaliation,
> a war without end, a war of revenge,
> a war of mutual annihilation,
> a "war of civilizations," recognizing the huts we all live in,
> should not our struggle be for a planetary peace . . .
> As God and Allah and Higher Power would have it?

Forgiveness

The ability to love, Bill often said, cannot exist without the ability to forgive, in every area from personal relationships to reconciliation among warring factions and nations.

> Forgiving involves at least two persons.
> If I insult you, you must retain, hold back until
> I sincerely ask you to forgive me.
> And then you must. I'm asking you to help me heal.
> You owe it to me out of faith and love to help me heal.
> If you refuse you wound yourself. Always is that danger.
> One who hurts causes the other to retaliate.
> You end up with two wounded.
> Healing, being reconciled is an action of
> give-and-take between us, a sign of God.

Addicts, mental and emotional patients, the enraged, all wounded psychologically, when forgiven and forgiving, become healthier in a community of equals, bound together as one by love. Believing that humans are created in God's image, then, doing community, sharing what we have with the other who lacks what it takes to live, is the essence of being human, which in turn reflects the glory of God.

> Most horrors of evil are committed by the non-forgiver.
> Why God born human, died human, and raised human?
>   To forgive us. So, does God love us!

At Mass, you know what's tragically sad is when we receive Holy Communion just for our own sake, without any thought of forgiving the one who hurt me, or asking to be forgiven, or not even thinking of reconciling. It's as if Jesus should never have ridden that pony into Jerusalem on that fateful day now called Palm Sunday.

Resurrection?

Just a fantasy!

Forgiving wipes away the psychic garbage
separating one from the enemy.
It gets unreal focus off a false self
and opens the real self to be itself to act nobly,
majestically, and even heroically.

To avoid confusion it must be emphasized that forgiveness and reconciliation are not the same thing. Forgiveness frees us to, moves us ahead beyond the past. Reconciliation helps us to restore relationships. Forgive first, then maybe reconcile if the other agrees. Achieving inner peace is the point. Takes two to fight. Takes one to forgive. Takes two to reconcile.

To forgive is to diffuse anger.
Forgiveness is the best revenge.
To forgive is not to let another rob you of your joy.
Resentment is a swamp forgiveness liberates us from.
Not to forgive sickens. To forget is naive.
To forgive and not forget teaches and is healthy.
To be like God, then I must forgive.

If I see you merely as a consumer to sell stuff to, or an enemy soldier to kill, or a minority to despise and exploit, I'm being worldly.

If I see you to love, to share myself with, to forgive and be forgiven by you, to respect you as an equal, to relate with you justly, then I'm being godly. God empowers me to hear God say: "It's in your hands, my child."

As hinted to above, needs and wants sometimes are but the two sides of the same coin. A common mantra on a labor picket line is: "No justice, No peace." It's saying, we need justice and want peace. In truth commissions established in nations after their civil war, its preface reads: "There will be no healing without justice, no justice without truth; no truth without full accountability." When these wants and needs are satisfied, then forgiveness may flow, the ultimate act of genuine love.

> Where there is no pardon, there is literally hell to pay.
> Violence begets violence. As for the offended,
> nonviolence is the only sane, healthy response.
> It's the abused giving the offender an opportunity
> to be forgiven and to be healed for peace.
> There is no way to forgiveness.
> Forgiveness is the way to heal broken bones.

> Ours is a second-chance religion.
> > Actually a seven-to-the-seventieth-power faith.

> The genius of Jesus insisting on forgiveness
> > is that it births a new life.

Peace is all about how do we forgive one another. First consider the consequences and we know we are grown up when we take responsibility for the consequences of those actions. When it is an injury, we become responsible for the healing of that wound, for righting that wrong.

> When forgiving is a foreign word, a word not
> > in our vocabulary, then what is the consequence?

Forgiving is like running water, like a river or the wind keeping the water moving on a lake. Running water refreshes, cleanses.

Not forgiving is like still water, like a cesspool, where the water becomes polluted and poisonous. Still water makes the drinker sick and it gets dirty and cannot cleanse.

Unforgiving is like a block of ice where nothing can live, wherein there is no movement. What goes unforgiven makes life freezing cold, where nothing moves.

Unforgiving has that consequence. When a person is hurt and does not forgive, a rage takes over, and when out of control that rage can cause untold injuries around the person not forgiving. It can regress to the point of even murder or suicide. Cold blood describes the unforgiving.

Look inside an addict and inevitably you will find an injury that has gone unforgiven. People get drunk and or high to kill a pain that will never go away until that wound is healed through forgiving the person who hurt you or asking forgiveness from the person whom you have wounded.

> First begin with God who can't help but forgive.
> God lives to forgive. Jesus died so we could get this
> life-and-death truth burned into our consciousness.
> When you do that then it gives you the courage to go
> to the person you're having trouble with privately,
> and try to get a true dialogue going,
> an exchange of what went on to cause the pain.
> When that happens, the guilt and pain
> dissolves and disappears and remains merely a memory.
>
> When we forgive, we are in fact, self-healing;
> we are inviting God into the process.
> Forgiving is an act of conversion to God's loving mercy;
> it's to experience God's compassion.
> Forgiving is turning from rage and resentment and seeking
> revenge to a state of peacefulness.
> We forgive in order not to become like the person
> who hurts us.

Protest and Nonviolence

Father Bill was most widely known for his involvement in protests. This involvement was grounded in his convictions about justice and love demanded by his faith. Beginning with civil rights protests in the 1960s, Bill continued protesting until the end of his life for justice and peace, in acts of civil disobedience that ledto almost 250 arrests. Early on, he was closely involved with Cesar Chavez, Dolores Huerta, and their United Farm Workers Union in the struggle to unionize to secure relief from backbreaking labor and to obtain rights and decent pay. One year, using his vacation time, Bill marched over a hundred miles with the farm workers from the Bay Area to Modesto to protest the Gallo Winery's opposition to the union. Chavez would stay at Bill's residence when he had received death threats, and the close relationship with the farm workers continued until Bill's death.

In the 1990s, Bill began protesting the School of the Americas, where foreign agents are trained in torture tactics. Often accompanying him at the annual protests in late November was his close friend, the actor Martin Sheen. It was his act of trespassing on government property in 2001 that led to his arrest, conviction, and a sentence of six months in the federal penitentiary at Atwater, California. Some of his reflections from that time in prison are included here.

In a final irony for this beloved lawbreaker, the number of people who came to his funeral at his beloved St. Joseph the Worker parish was so great that police had to be summoned to handle the overflow of traffic.

United Farm Workers—A Tactic or a Way of Life —Unitarian Church, January 19, 1975

I'm not sure if I'm personally qualified to speak on behalf of the UFW in their Non- Violent Direct Action struggle for self-determination.

On the one hand, I have experienced abuse, insults and threats on the picket line in the city and on the ranches from the growers' goons, store managers, and some consumers—and threats and isolation from authorities in my own church. I don't say this for your sympathy.

This experience qualifies me, but on the other hand another experience casts the shadow of doubt on my qualifications to speak on nonviolence. A would-be robber, his face concealed by a stocking mask, got into our priest's house and announced: "We have the house surrounded . . . don't call the police" . . . To make a long story short . . . I threw him down and then threw him out . . . That makes me no less violent than he was—probably more so.

In 1968, Cesar Chavez went on his first publicized fast because members of his own union were so discouraged that all their nonviolent direct action efforts seemed to be fruitless. Some people in the Farm Workers movement said, "Nonviolent as long as it works." Finally an example of violence on the picket line. A labor contractor at 5 AM, Monday morning two months ago, drove his bus to 12th and Jefferson in West Oakland. A group of us was waiting when we approached his bus. He had maybe fifteen goon guards waiting for us, each holding a lead pipe in their hands. We surrounded the bus in the hope that workers would not board this particular bus headed for a ranch that was on strike.

As this was happening a group of young people whom I've never seen before appeared from the back, charged the bus, and began to break the red lights. The police intervened and arrested one of the assailants. I said to myself, what's going on? Goons hit people and things, not the UFW. As it turned out the UFW repudiated this group. This kind of action was never allowed. The UFW would not even put up "bail" for this young group's release.

The UFW is preaching a gospel that nonviolence is not a tactic; as a tactic it fails, but as a way of life, it's power. If all the enemy can do then is kill you, that's a greater problem for them actually than for the one open to being killed. Those who fear death judge people who live nonviolence as being insane. But of the two which one really is insane?

Nonviolence is not somebody else's thing. It's my challenge and yours. Are you married? Is your relationship nonviolent? We're all political. How do you feel about Nixon? CIA? The Pentagon?

Now you can sense how farm workers feel about any of the non-union, rich, powerful employers. The ultimate violence is for the farm worker to become a company man.

The UFW is the only movement (at this time) in America that is doing nonviolence, using the most potent weapons available to poor people: the strike and the boycott. Their poverty is their best weapon, as they have turned their poverty into peace.

The UFW is the only game in town that is saying: "We gain control over our lives by nonviolence."

And so it is; Jesus flew into the faces of the Pharisees and of the wealthy with the story of the rich man and Lazarus. The goal of life is not the pursuit of happiness, but to be blessed; that is to say, to be like God, to live in the presence of God, to struggle to make his "kingdom come" to "take up your cross and follow me" and that is where happiness, a profound joy, is experienced, not as a goal, but as a consequence, and no amount of wealth can be substituted for this. To strive to be blessed, to live like Jesus, that's what saves us from emptiness, loneliness, depression, rage, and isolation. In the world of finance and politics, they say you have to be well connected. Jesus says make sure first whom you're connected to . . . and if not with God, then any other kind is pretending and substituting, with utter misery as a lasting consequence. But to acknowledge God within, that has an everlasting consequence. Happy is in the pursuit of justice.

The Lazarus life, "the thrown away" life, is the crucifying experience, but then life flip-flops and it's the once miserable Lazarus who becomes far more wealthy than even the rich man dreamed . . .

Editor's note:
[The following are excerpts from Father Bill's defense against charges of trespassing at the Livermore Lab held before the

judge at Livermore Municipal Court.]

If you do not own great wealth, some medium of communication, are not a public and popular figure, and, after voting for policies and politicians who work for peace through disarmament; if when the telephone, e-mail, and letter-writing seem to have no braking power to slow up Armageddon, then unusual, extraordinary means must be taken to reach the conscience of the citizen.

Civil disobedience, I have come to believe, is the only means available to communicate to our society what society allows to be done in its name. It is even necessary to do civil disobedience to let our public know how all of us civilians are intentionally kept ignorant of the unimaginably destructive nuclear bombs on the drawing boards at the Livermore Lawrence laboratory.

If a free society is to remain free, then essential to its existence is the right of the people to be informed in order for that people to knowledgeably and intelligently decide what is best for its ultimate interest. Secrecy is the terrible nemesis of democracy.

Writing letters to Congress, to the news media are important; if most Lab activities are secret, what is there with which to inform the media? As a society, we feel Mafia secrecy is a national scandal; in the megatons then is the Pentagon–UC Livermore Lab secrecy, a scandal?

Civil disobedience in this situation becomes the highest act of patriotism. To love one's brothers and sisters enough to risk reputation, career, fines, and imprisonment to attempt to reveal the evil of nuclear pollution, then it is morally most highly commendable.

> Breaking unjust laws is breaking the chains that denigrate, disrespect, and humiliate. And the more often, and the greater numbers of us who break the law, the more hope we gain to overcome the forces of slavery and win that dignity, respect and rights that are ours as persons,
> and as your children . . . God of Power,
> give us the heart and the vision to do your will. Amen

F&I=1 (Oneness)

"The Father and I are one"... you just heard it. Now, if Jesus can say it, then why can't I? Why can't you? Well, because you and I are not Jesus Christ, it is argued. To be one with the Father you have to be Jesus Christ? Why can't anybody be one with the Father? Jesus said in the gospel: if I can be one with the Father, so can you. So, how come I am not one with the Father, that is to say, if I'm not, then how come I'm not?

Evil is not knowing the answer to why the Father and I are not one. Evil is not knowing anything about God. Evil is not knowing anything about myself or about you.

Evil you can't define, but you can describe it; like the Supreme Court said about pornography: you know it when you see it.

It's evil that comes between the Father and me and there are as many evil things as there are things, for when a thing is not perfect, then it contains evil, and the more incomplete it is the more evil it is. So, the more evil between the Father and I the farther apart we are. So, about the best I can say about the Father and me (and it's like this with a lot of couples) we are more or less one with one another.

Evil is something that is not there: evil is an empty glass... Evil is a camera with no film... A creek bed without a creek... A meadow without flowers and grass. Grapes without sugar...

Evil is a body without life... A mind without thought... A heart without feeling... art without beauty, music without sound. A day without sobriety. A bombed out federal building, a broken love affair, a failed marriage.

Evil always looks good until it is revealed for what it really is. A suitcase bulging with 100 dollar bills looks terrific until you discover it's stolen.

There are structural evils; today's global economy called neoliberalism, designed by multinational corporations and enforced by Congress that would remove all laws that protect most people from corporate greed; for example, to take away Social Security. It's a financial system that talks about "disposable" people in our world; those who do not produce or consume; they are to be let go and die, and if they don't accept their fate, then more prisons are to be built to remove them as obstacles to an economy that will make the wealthy, wealthier beyond their dreams... A horrendous evil that today rules the marketplace. The more structured evil is, the more destructive its consequences; for example, slavery; it may have been formally abolished more than one hundred years ago, but informally it still exists in the virulent form of racism, unjust immigrant laws, and sexism that constructs glass ceilings, that makes the body a sexual object, and pays women half as much as it pays men for the same job.

There is no end to structural evil, but the point here is that its effects on people can be the reason why the people are not one with the Father as Jesus was. This system is so seductive that it promises everybody riches when it knows that to thrive it needs cheap labor and a jobless class to keep workers competing for the same jobs, thus lowering wages.

So what do we do with this blob, this barrier, this block, this fog between the Father and us?

We have to admit to it, name it, describe if not define it, unmask it, detoxify or contain evil, using love as our counter force and hope as an impetus that it can be overcome. And the first step is to yield, submit to the Father, to God, and admit that the evil is too strong for me to overcome, and only with God's help is it possible not to be wasted. When that happens there occurs instantaneous union with God; the evil becomes the grace to be one with the Father.

Jesus said: "the Father and I are one." how could he say such a ridiculous thing: Unless, evil is whatever lessens relations between us, whatever denies or suppresses one or the other's power to be in a relationship completely, and if there was no barrier to Jesus' relationship to God, then of course he could say: "the Father and I are one."

And so can you.
And so can I.

> God of light, you reveal to us how the forces of darkness
> would blind us to your love for us . . .
> you will all your children to live in dignity and with respect,
> whatever is fit to being human;
> respect, giving the honor due to a person,
> simply because they are human.

God of Justice, when law fails,
indeed disrespects our right to respect
and denies our right to dignity;
such law is a curse and deserves to be broken.

Catholic Labor Committee Breakfast 5/23/03

The hardest work in the universe has to be organizing, not only the most valuable, but also the most satisfying. Organizing is an art, no less challenging than writing, painting or sculpting.

Unions are called to organize every worker to see
to it that corporations live justly with their workers.
All must work together to create a domination-free order,
or as Jesus proclaimed in the Mountain Sermon . . .

[Editor's note: For a number of years, Father Bill participated in protests against the School of the Americas, located at Fort Benning, Georgia. The School of the Americas, now known by the euphemistic Western Hemisphere Institute for Security Cooperation, trains operatives from foreign lands to participate in torture and other acts of terror. Its graduates have participated in numerous massacres, the most notorious being the murder of six Jesuit priests, their housekeeper, and her daughter in El Salvador in 1989.

Father Bill was arrested before at this place. In 2002, along with other protestors, including another priest, Father Louis Vitale of San Francisco, he was brought to trial for trespassing into an area forbidden by the military. His opposition to the school was intensified by the fact that he had personally visited some of the countries where the graduates operated, and had talked to their torture victims. He knew others who had fled to the U.S. The following is an extract from his testimony in court.]

Federal Court, Columbus, Georgia, July 8–12, 2002

Sir, [Father bill refused to use the term "Your Honor"] my pleading not guilty began in 1997 when Father Roy Bourgeois spoke on the West Coast about graduates of the School of the Americas returning to their respective countries to torture, mutilate, and disappear their own people.

Since 1980 I have been visiting peasants, workers, church and health workers in Nicaragua, El Salvador, Guatemala, Chiapas, and refugee camps in Honduras, where graduates of the SOA have wreaked havoc. Repeatedly did they tell stories of their own soldiers terrorizing their own populations.

This court contemplates sentences of six months in prison and fines up to $5,000 dollars for us defendants. My question to this court is: for the identical offense at the Federal building in Oakland, California, eight of us citizens, for protesting the United States bombing in Afghanistan, were sentenced to six hours of community service, no fines, no probation. Can we defendants expect judicial equity in this court as well?

This court has the power to close down this camp for terrorists and allow real democracy to be taught in these countries where land-starved peasants and slave-driven workers struggle to live free from attacks by their own soldiers trained here.

This court can shut the school down that has been operating since the end of World War II, when the U.S. Army recruited a high-ranking Nazi SS officer in charge of Eastern Europe operations to teach U.S. personnel in the evil art of terror. Such is the legacy for a hemisphere that has been soaking in the blood of dissidents, politicians, health workers, peasants, children, mothers, union organizers, intellectuals, catechists, priests, nuns and three bishops.

History will judge the judges who cover up for the Pentagon, who render the harshest penalties allowed by law on trespassers, not so incidentally to intimidate any future protesters from crossing the line next November 17. But, our tribe increases. This court's severity only fuels the fire of protest. We must be grateful for your help.

Our friends do pity our fate. However, that is nothing compared to how your grandchildren, indeed their whole generation, will regard the cover-up on this court, in a sinister partnership with the Pentagon, with horror and disgust. It will be known when the truth is exposed about this more than 50-year-old camp that trains foreign terrorists who crush their own people in order for multinational companies to be safe to profit from virtual slave labor. This court has for years been pimping for the Pentagon and as any professional pimp does, covers up the crimes of his prostitutes. This court and military conspire to cover up this camp training terrorists. This cover-up of the crimes of violence taught at the School of America, compared to the Catholic Bishops cover-up of child sexual molestation makes their hideous crime look like some backroom illegal poker game.

Judge, may I suggest a way out of this judicial logjam? Sentence me to study at this infamous school, for me to emerge after six months to tell the world: Indeed the new Institute has amended its ways and teaches only nonviolence and democracy to its students. Not to sentence me there will leave the world asking: what is the Pentagon and this court hiding from the people? [*Editor's note:* After discussing this proposal with the School of the Americas Watch Committee, it was decided not to make this offer, as it would be playing into the SOA's hands.]

Trashing the Dead

May, I tell you of an incident when a nonviolent force got into the face of a violent force . . . the nonviolent force was victorious . . . morally.

On November 23, 2003, an over 11,000 motley group of mostly Catholics, clergy, nuns, and lay people processed in a funeral march in front of the gates at Fort Benning, Georgia. Accompanying us were Quakers, Unitarians, Jews, Protestants, Moslems, atheists, vegetarians, miscellaneous pacifists, unclassified idealists, followers of Gandhi, King, and Jesus, all peace people, all sweet damn fools for peace, led in song by Pete Seeger, with messages from Susan Sarandon, Martin Sheen, Joan Baez, Bonnie Raitt, Jackson Browne, Sister Helen Prejean, author of *Dead Man Walking*, and others.

The entrance to the fort that houses the infamous School of the Americas is a broad two-lane street, about two football fields long. The funeral march was organized with mourners eight abreast, each carrying white, foot-and-a-half-size crosses, each with the name of a person murdered or massacred by a graduate from this school of assassins, ranging from a pregnant woman to an 87-year-old man. All non-combatant innocents. From the stage a cantor chanted a name; then hearing it we raised our crosses and responded: "Presente . . . we honor you; we remember you!" . . .

This procession moved for about three to four hours around in a huge two-blocks-long circle. Meanwhile about 40 protesters slipped off to the side, to "cross over the line," to be arrested for trespassing onto army property. Incidentally, but not so incidentally, the soldiers had mounted behind the fenced-off entrance large boom box–type speakers that were loud enough to be heard a mile away, playing patriotic songs. The obvious intention was to drown out the speeches that preceded the funeral procession. Some of us complained, threatening to sue the fort on grounds of interfering with our constitutional right of free speech. Eventually the colonel in charge ordered the microphone to be shut off.

During the march, the mourners began to insert their crosses into the chain link fence that blocked the entrance into the fort. At about 4:30 in the afternoon the procession began to wind down; the media had departed. The fence took on the look of a wall of white

At this time about 30 soldiers appeared, shouting at us to move back from the fence or be arrested. They began ferociously to tear the crosses down from off the fence, tossing them into a pile, then stomping on them. The thin wood breaking under their boots sounded like bones cracking.

A garbage truck soon backed up to this trashing, where the fence surrendered its wall of sacred symbols. Then the soldiers began unceremoniously to heave the broken crosses into the truck's bed. As it filled up soldiers again stomped on the crosses, crushing them further to look like a pile of kindling wood. Some witnessing the soldiers' rage began chanting "Peace, Shalom, Pax," having an effect of easing the shock this desecration stirred as our eyes filled with tears. Others horrified at this brutalization of the memory of the martyred simply walked away.

The soldiers in their frenzy, systematically smashing these simple icons, made me wonder if this is what they would be doing to peacemakers if they weren't aware that "The whole world is watching." Their hard cold glares indicated they perceived us as terrorists, anti-American, anti-patriots, the enemy.

We were witnessing an act of fury; the same fanatical behavior they teach young men and women not only in our own army, but specially selected personnel from the armies of the Americas. Most trainees now come from war-torn Columbia.

The soldiers seemed to be acting out in an attempt to obliterate maybe an unconscious guilt, as well as the memory of murdering and massacring the innocent victims of their training . . . it looked like some kind of false purge.

Unforgettable! Witnessing this Trashing of the Dead. We eventually all walked away feeling what Liz Fuentes articulated: "They just don't know what they are doing!"

Does this nation know what the School of the Americas/WHSIC is doing in our name?

Jonah the Crank—January 26, 2003 . . . Yr. "B"

Jonah House is a Catholic Christian commune located in a cemetery. It was once the caretaker's residence in Baltimore, Maryland. The community calls itself "Plowshares," honoring Isaiah pleading with the Israelites to beat their swords into plowshares. Founded by Phil Berrigan and his wife, Elizabeth McAlister, they named the house after Jonah, the prophet. Their mission was to warn America against its own addiction to violence that is driving this nation to nuclear destruction. Unlike the citizens of Nineveh, U.S. citizens pay little heed to this modern Jonah and his plowshare fellows, with the media shrugging off his civil disobedience as passé.

Jonah of the Bible apparently did not have Phil's ingratiating personality and captivating smile. The original Jonah in social justice circles might be viewed as a whacko-crank, a whining rebel, a mean-spirited loner; he gloated over the prospect of God destroying his vile enemies, "who can't distinguish right from wrong." People with no conscience need a good comeuppance by way of a good put-down, Jonah figured. When God showed mercy, Jonah showed tantrum. So enraged at God was Jonah, he felt like just giving up and dying. Jonah now had to return to face his own people. What credibility had he left with them if God did not punish the wicked heathen who let their city get worse than a Sodom and Gomorrah? Jonah even took his rage out on one pathetic tree. It had wilted from no watering and died. This deprived Jonah of the little comfort that its shade would have provided. He was furious at God's nature, which seemed to be siding with God's unrepenting friends.

In populace Nineveh was near Berkeley's count, but in size the place was probably larger than Oakland. Jonah figured it to be a waste of his time to go tramping from end to end warning the dwellers of the coming ruin of their city unless they repented. Apparently, the people turned out to listen, to agree with the prophet, that their moral degradation had sunken disastrously. They reached thankfully to Jonah's preachments and began to repent by reversing their lifestyles.

That shocked Jonah. They denied him of deriving some self-righteous pleasure that revenge brings. Jonah exhibited a kind of political schizophrenia—he mirrored a liberal and conservative streak.

Liberals leave the room when the fight starts. Jo' left Nineveh. Jo' could have said with Will Rogers, "I belong to no organized party, I'm a democrat." Then there is his conservative bent. A good liberal is a dead one. He wanted the Ninevites dead. Jo' never computed the damage to the environment that destruction would cause. Nor did he have any compassion for the good people of the city.

There is no end to conjecturing about this city and its Nemesis-turned-Savior. The truth oozing from the myth is eminently clear. God's mercy is as magnanimous as God's justice is severe. What the people may have deserved is punishment, but by turning their lives around they experienced compassionate forgiveness. Hubris can be deflated with humility. The mad prophet learned too from the people of God's marvelous mercy.

Many are the Jonah types today in all our cities warning our rulers not to war against the innocents of Iraq. We are challenged to repent as the Ninevites were. Phil Berrigan awards with everlasting peace, birthing thousands of Jonahs. —The OD

Prison

The following writings are mostly excerpted from the six months in 2002–2003 when Father Bill was incarcerated at the U.S. penitentiary in Atwater, California, for trespassing at the School of the Americas at Fort Benning, Georgia. As was often the case, Bill questioned his own motives, wondering if accolades and ego were getting the better of him and displacing faith. Always keenly interested and open to everyone, he became well acquainted with many fellow prisoners, and enjoyed retelling their varied stories, while drawing whatever moral he found in the experience. He even started a Bible reading "lectionary" group, a sort of substitute for the interdenominational one at home that he met with every week.

THE HEART SPEAKS more eloquently than does the mind. St. Augustine: to love is to know. Aquinas countered; to know is to love. Both speak a truth. The mind designs rules, regulations and laws. When the heart overrules the mind, and breaks the law, the heart is obeying a higher law, of conscience, higher than the Supreme Court or the Pope. The heart hears God. The mind hears man. When the heart speaks the person knows peace, the hungry are fed, homeless sheltered, sick cared for. The mind may produce food and architect houses and scientists discover medicines. When the two are divorced, the mind dominates and justifies punishing its enemy to the point of killing. (Federal Prison, December 2002)

Goodbye, For Now! —Bulletin from Twenty-Third Sunday in Ordinary Time, September 2002 . . . Yr. 'A'

The Federal court has managed to reroute my life's journey for the next six months into the joint called United States Penitentiary, Atwater, seven miles north of Merced. I drove by the 23,000 pop. town the week before last. The prison is a couple of miles east of Atwater, or is it Nowater?! None is observable; no creeks, no rivers, no lakes. Atwater could be called Dry Land.

Father Crespin [Father Bill's colleague at St. Joseph the Worker in Berkeley] has asked that I keep in touch with you by way of continuing to write each week this theme part, or what I call "Billy Bull."

My belief, indeed my understanding, of why I decided to risk this sentencing, is to contribute my small part to the struggle to have the American people notice that our government runs a military camp for terrorists. Here at Fort Benning, Georgia, Latin American soldiers are trained in the techniques of torture and rape as a fear tactic, as well as panicking a population by disappearing, assassinating, and murdering the nation's prominent leaders in religion, labor, and medicine. Since 1946, the once School of the Americas is now called The Western Hemisphere Institute for Security and Cooperation (WHISC)—rhetoric for a high-tech camp for training professional killers. Congress last year made this name-change, pressured by the 11 years of public demonstrations focused on this house of horrors. How is it justified? This academy of assassins trains other countries' military to war on their own people, making their oligarchies safe, as well as making Third World nations secure for U.S. multi-billionaire companies to exploit cheap resources and labor. Such an operation needs to be top secret. That's why any U.S. citizens risking arrest is being punished to the max the law allows, in order to silence any opposition to this scandal.

"Crossing the line" at the Fort last November 17 with 90 others and convicted with 35 others last July 12 was more than an act of simple civil disobedience, merely to get the media's attention to the Pentagon's Nazi-inspired practice of this Black Art. This simple act was entirely consistent with the over 33 years and 224 arrests and countless more times I've trespassed onto government and private properties to address a particular issue of injustice. My simple belief is an unjust law is no law and deserves no respect, but ought to be broken. Being a slow learner, it took me almost four decades to get that it's not only one's civic duty, but an honorable act. With enough of us doing that, then that law gets quietly dropped. I used to think "keep the rules and the rules will keep you" made sense. My experience showed this slogan for the serfs was designed to keep the lord secure. But what does one do when The Man, bishop, boss, or judge, has the power to punish if you don't conform to his inhuman expectations. I learned to go outside of his box. I live in ways foreign to his mentality. He enforces his rules couched in legal terms.

To live nonviolently, opposing his way with direct actions, confuses The Man. He reacts the only way he knows how, by means of sanctions such as firings, fines, and jailing. Meanwhile, his enterprises become threatened by people having nothing to do with him or his business, whether it be commercial, political, or religious. This is all sooo gospel!

Do I resent Judge "6-months-max" Faircloth, who fears us all who come to Fort Benning to protest in his jurisdiction? Mallon Faircloth, or as I call him in fun, "Misjudge Mallet Dirtyrag," would win if I hated him. I forgive him. I pity him. His being a toady of the military and all. But resent him? If I did then he'd have won.

You, Saint Joseph the Workers, make my priest's heart. I'll miss you when not communing with new friends, wearing those funny-looking jump suits. Goodbye, for now, "til the next "Billy Bull" . . . —The OD

Getting Real—November 3, 2002

Last November I was out walking with a few friends; police estimated about 11,000. Fort Benning military police at the entrance to the School of the Americas (WHISC) with bullhorns warned us that to cross over an invisible line we would be arrested for trespass. Ninety of us wanted to call upon the commander of the school where the United States trains terrorists. We crossed over, were arrested and booked and given "ban and bar" letters that stated that we were subject to six months in prison and a $5,000 fine and released.

Last July, 37 of the 90 went on trial. The magistrate gaveled: guilty. I and 28 got the six months, the others lesser sentences.

Between then and now, many people have affirmed our action of protest and have been alarmed at the severity of the sentence. For all these months people have been huzzaing, thumbs-upping, cheering, well-wishing, and blessing our decision to speak truth to endless power.

Oh! Gosh! Gee whiz! Golly me! These kudos make me out to be somebody. As my head swells to an eight, I think oh! oh! Am I'm taking my self too seriously? So I pray: God, who loves a fat head? Won't you do something? And God answers down deep in the heart of my heart: OK.

Two days later the warden assigns me to work as an orderly. "Your job, and everyone works in my prison, is to not wash, not clean, but scour every sink (11); every urinal (5) every toilet (12), and every shower stall (15)."

In today's gospel what Jesus taught was to look at your official teachers. See how they say one thing and do the opposite. Tell you to go offer your miserable lives up, and they live in comfort, shopping at the best stores for their finest and latest fashion. They strut. At least our politicians pretend humility around election days. This great teacher's secret is to go from the known (religious leader's hypocrisy) to the unknown, the life of humility for us followers.

Humility is being free to let go of what I want and pursue what I need. I want a Lexus, but a bike will get me around town anywhere fast. Humility frees me to say no to what I want: sex, drugs, elegant dining, and luxurious living. Humility frees me to live simply that the poor can simply live. I want to possess. The more I have, the more I'll be happy. It makes me obsess on money, when not on women. The plan after my release is to live in Brazil, Costa Rica, and Ireland, where they can have all the above without having to share it with Uncle Sam in taxes.

Freedom, the quality that makes us human, above the animal, like the angel, depends on being our authentic selves, conscious of how deeply connected we are to one another. Passionate about serving primarily the unabled. In a word a humble person is the most joyful, the kindest, the least phony. The humble attracts like a magnet. The proud repels like a bad smell.

Federal Penitentiary, Atwater, California, September 10, 2002. 8:30 AM: The Send Off:

In his room prior to going out to meet his supporters, Father Bill wrote in pencil:

"In my most private moments totally alone and the demons of fear sprang awake. Remembering how Jesus nagged, more than "Follow me," was—Faith—fear not—have faith. So, when the butterflies rose in my stomach, I resorted to Help, Help, Help. First, all the panicking-type fear left. Then I go to the church and find over a hundred friends applauding, and too complimentary speeches."

On the steps of St. Joseph's Father Bill said goodbye. Then, he entered a car with Delores Huerta, a friend, and his sister Mary. He drove past Berkeley City Hall with a "PRAY FOR THE WARDEN—FREE FATHER BILL" banner prepared by his alcoholic/drug recovery group members. He was followed by a caravan of seven cars.

From 11:40 to noon, a small group of United Farm Workers and Father Bill's friends have met in the parking lot outside the prison and are waiting for him when he arrives at Atwater Penitentiary. They hold a prayer circle and blessing. There are federal employees with cameras filming their every move. Father Bill walks up to the front door and knocks. There is no answer. He finds this strange and knocks again. No answer. After several minutes two prison employees come out the door. Father Bill said, "I'm here to turn myself in." The men said, "We thought it was a demonstration to rescue you, and the prison had to be "locked down." Father Bill waved goodbye and entered the prison, "fearless—with friends and God, you can do anything, I discovered all over again." The heavy door slammed shut.

The following is taken from his notes written in pencil. He speaks about the small group of friends outside. This caused the whole facility to shut down. All work stopped. The Correctional Officer said, "We thought the demonstrators might shoot." Not until friends left did prison routine begin again.

The first Correctional Officer, a baby-faced young man who walked me into the process center, said, "Wha dija do?" I said, "Trespass to shut down the SOA." "That's wrong, Father, you're giving us Catholics a bad name."

I was treated with particular courtesy. The guard at the gate when I was being led from the "Hole" (maximum Security) to the Camp, remarked, "The Camp! You just got here! You're the quickest processed I've ever seen." The guys tell me usually it takes four-five days to be transferred from the Hole to the Camp. I attributed this to friends and my sister's earlier calls to the chaplain alerting the administrator of my heart condition and who knows what else the "advocates" said.

The Camp. A "Costco" space including a ceiling of pipes, a pitched roof supported by three I-beam pillars, air conditioned, and a concrete floor. Down each side of the "hall" are two rows of bunks bedding down 120 inmates. The center space has a pinball table, a soccer game, and eight round tables where guys talk, play cards, and watch silent TV with head phones. The bathroom has an adequate number of urinals and toilet stalls. There are three micowaves available for food purchased at the commissary. And exercise and laundry room are available.

Outside are picnic tables on a lawn, a baseball diamond, a track for jogging as well as two basketball courts.

In a separate building is a dining room, a chapel, rooms for TV watching, and a clothes and bedding room

"The Big I"—pure institution; order, control, autonomous—guards making a living. They're "guarded."In the Big I everyone's a prisoner, even the warden and beyond.

9/11 Day 1

Breakfast—Accidentally met Dr. Bill, joined by Dr. Ray, who gave me his water bottle. 11:45 AM—Meeting with Mr. Dreyer requested my meds taken by the two docs at receiving. I'm informed I'll be punished if my friends send faxes to the Pen's fax (duh) "So, tell them not to"—"duh."

Waiting at the Commissary for toiletries. Chris and I begin to talk—15 months left on his conviction for medical marijuana, growing it in Humboldt County from a wave of sweeps by the Drug Enforcement Agency in California. His legal defense: arguing from the concept of the fundamental right of a patient to use the treatment of their choice and the duty and right of the state to regulate the health, safety, and welfare of its citizens. In 1994 Chris had a severely injured spinal cord—and was paralyzed until surgery inserted two steel rods for support—said he used marijuana to ease the pain.

Mail Call—two letters and two postcards on the 2nd eve, a bro yelled: "Hey! You just go here!" I told the whole world, "Just four pieces?"

9/12

Bible Study—led by semi-Fundie doc—so sure of himself and his understanding of the Bible. Lied to live. It was about Sarah being his sister and not his wife, so the Pharaoh wouldn't kill him. It was OK for the doc to let the lies go. I said, "There are two kinds of lies."[Bill didn't elaborate, instead he told the story of Joe] Joe, "I never heard this stuff in eight years of Catholic school and an altar boy." At 23 Joe got 20 years. He was betrayed by his best friend. "I can't forgive him." To get here the Feds gave him a bus ticket and 8 hours to visit with his wife—she's now pregnant.

He (Joe) never snitched for personal integrity reasons. He's been in seven pens and could walk the yard alone untouched because inmates could trust him. Remorse for selling drugs and hurting family.

Rev. Jim—so full of God. His path from alcoholism to prison ministry in God opening up doors. He had problems with my questions, e.g., "Do the inmates teach you about God?" No response, except what God does for him. For me it's a turn-off because it's so personal in him and doesn't relate to mine.

Mary called—to visit this weekend—a real lift in spirit—first excitement, the tie that springs joy.

Ray—Atwater is the model for building a rehab—toughest one yet. Food is nutritional, fresh, tasty, simple.

Tracy—engineer—designed homes for his bro. He said, "This is staff's career, the jokes on them. For us it's only temporary."

9/13

Doc Bill's story—He had a chain of clinics in the Central Valley outside of Fresno (13). Plus a research center—½ of his patients were Medi-Cal—Convicted of Medi-Cal fraud—he lost eight million dollars fighting his case—a 10-year sentence.

Mail call—7 letters

9/14—Saturday

11:50 PM, "Jo Jo," the Correctional Officer (CO), who "hates inmates" comes into the "middle." This area is surrounded by three sides of bunks, where two TVs are on forever. He orders the TV's "off." "Why?" the viewers ask. "They've been on for three months." Strickly speaking, Jo Jo is correct, but why wait until midnight, when the regs read 10 PM for lights and TVs off. Jo Jo repeats. The guys call for the Lieutenant. Jo Jo refuses and himself pulls the plugs to the TVs. From then until 9/15 at 1:30 AM, the guys start yelling vulgarities at Jo Jo. Soon after midnight Jo Jo begins the mandated count. He goes around the three sides of the hall several times miscounting until the 9th round until he gets it right. The catcalling increased. Around 1:15 AM, the fire alarm goes off. All are ordered outside. About 1:45 AM a CO tongue-lashes the campers with vulgar obscene language, how this behavior over unplugging the TV is all BS and the trouble caused her to report the incident to the warden. The mini-riot is over. I was back in the 5th grade, except the nuns never showed rage or talked dirty.

9/15 Sunday

Lunch with Topy from Hawaii, works gardening and walks six miles a day, a transfer from Lompoc where the camp has so many more programs. He wishes he was back there. Five years to go. Very expensive for his wife and child to visit.

Musing:

When bored, depressed, generally feeling low, it occurred to me going to sleep, to do whatever is creative. For example, writing. For me the exercise takes me out of the stalled self—it makes for movement. Change is what jolts me out of the duh-state. Creating, e.g., painting, reading, gardening, carpentering, a movie, whatever, makes me rather than attending to the still-self, attend to "the other." That makes me move off me and to another. Attending to

God is never boring. Very hard with distraction; the constant challenge. With despair dispatched only sleep can break the trance of the exciting.

49er game—gallery reacts with Ed: descriptive expletives.

10/05
Received 58 letters: 37 from children.

10/10
A bag of cookies, shampoo, Dove skin cream arrived on my bunk. Who? I asked several. Word got to me it was Lee. Going to return the gifts from "I don't need." I was told they were gifts from "friends." I was deeply moved by their quiet generosity. I call Lupe the George Patton of the Banos—a workaholic is good and bad—bad because he's such a moral force to work hard, and good he does so much of your work.

Letters—received 47 letters from adults; 15 from 4th graders. Inmates suggest I have my own mail bag. *[Editor's note.* Bill answered every one of his letters.]

Began a "Lectionary group" stylized on our home group—an agnostic, a Sikh, and six Catholics—a roaring success. Doc Bill, a fundie tried to control—he left about three-fourths of the hour. It works when individuals talk about their own experience with next Sunday's readings. It's coming down to Doc Dan and Doc Bill having a Protestant fundamentalist group and one Catholic group.

> Prison is being shut in from getting up and going—meeting with all guys night and day, 24/7 and no women, only to gawk at some on visitation day. Prison is restriction to narrow space where time seems to say "No Tomorrow."

> Prison is wondering about your family, how are my friends doing; how can I do without them.

> Prison is living with 128 guys under one roof, in an almost crowded one-room warehouse-type building with three walls with double rows of bunk beds, each with its own 1"x 2" x 3" locker.

> Prison is listening to the noise of TV, shouts of guys playing ping pong. Flopping rubber slippers to the showers.

Prison is missing you. Prison is bearing the humiliation of the guard whose attitude is it's us versus them.

Prison is how do you humanize the inhuman?

Prison is waiting for Godot.

Outside, I wished time would not speed so fast, inside it drags boringly slow.

Fear is a factor to struggle with.
Lover Jesus insisted it was taking on the struggle itself
that brings intimacy. Trusting God,
suspicious of the world's seductive promise
of glory and power, confident Jesus lives
at the heart of my heart and will lead me
to Bethlehem where I with
the shepherds will come to adore.

Federal Prison—December 1, 2002
In this Christmas season the world celebrates God becoming intimate with His People, so much as to be one of us.
We praise you, God, our father who that first Christmas loved Joseph and Mary to trust your son to be born their son.
We bless you God, our father, who this Christmas season loves this Joseph and Maricella, young Mary, enough to entrust your daughter to be born their daughter, Amanda, to love all she meets as Jesus loves us.
Amen

Prison is no fun, nothing delightful happens. Pleasure is against the "regs." Joy is quite possible. I have known it when meditating; I have felt the deepest joy of knowing God is present, even in the repugnant behavior of the authorities, who, sadly, have no joy in the expressions on their faces, or words, or maybe in their lives.

We humans are desperate for joy. It's as needed as air. Too often substitutes are made. Pleasure is sought in its stead. How you get to feel good is the common quest. Dancing, sports, movie going and the like promise fun. Food, sex, work, clothes, money, bring a high, as maybe drugs and alcohol. I counsel addicts to suggest their pursuit of the ultimate high is but a substitute for the ecstatic Communion with God.

> When I am in the present, now, present myself
> to the Presence of God, I may experience
> the profound joy in offering myself as a present.

[Editor's note: Regarding prison Father Bill quoted Mark Twain: "This confinement gives added meaning to meaningless and waste, i.e., to stupidity. If you ever wish to observe the dregs of society, go visit any prison to view the changing of the guard." Then Bill said, "But, I'd do it again if it would contribute to slamming shut the door to that School of Infamy (The School of the Americas). Incarceration here is being a victim of that School for Terrorists. I've been imprisoned and "disappeared"; fair game on this end of the spectrum as the graduates of the school victimize their enemies by jailing and disappearing their victims. We are in solidarity with the terrorist's enemies who are the church workers, labor organizers, and the peasants of the Americas.]

> Trusting God opens a life unpredictable, full of adventure;
> however, enjoying every comfort all the time.

October 2002

Some ways become so narrow they end in a jungle. Here the lost may find their way out by listening to the murmurs of the heart speaking of the way that opens to freedom. Maybe being lost means we be found in the heart of God.

In prison the two baits that got most inmates caught were greed and gluttony, or money and drugs. Money can be very addictive. People will steal, lie, betray even kill for money. It's a fist-clencher morally. Fists so clenched that they can't let go—in prison many are unclenching, letting go, converting to freedom.

Lent is letting go. If it's wrath, walk away. Is lust eye candy? Honor the body as sacred, love as Jesus loved by caring, respecting, freeing oneself to be loved, cared for, and respected.

Lent is developing the power of discipline, of self-control of the appetites. Patience is power. Humility works wonders. Pray to believe. Believe to love. Love to serve. Live forever. Easter is the proof.

Recycling a Wheat Germ

Wheat bread is a favorite of most, other than the allergic. It's quite simple to bake. Take a cup full of wheat grain, pulverize, add yeast and water, let rise, bake it, and voila! A loaf of wheat bread!

Jesus uses a grain of wheat to teach a simple yet profound truth about our selves, besides predicting his own death and resurrection . . . "unless a grain of wheat fall to the ground and die, it remains just a grain of wheat; but if it dies it produces much fruit."

Let's fantasize for a moment that this grain of wheat is a metaphor for our egos.

Doing time in prison I was assigned to scour toilets, urinals, showers, sinks, and mirrors. Mindless humble work, but time for reflection, meditation and especially observing men in their narcissistic staring at themselves in the mirror for the longest time.

I thought women were vain with spending inordinate time before mirrors with their dabbing and daubing any variety of cosmetics.

In seminary it was drummed into our vanity-leaning souls that a minute before the mirror was sufficient for the purpose of face washing or shaving. To glance in a store window to check one's refection was nothing but vainglorious behavior, a tsk tsk on the morality scale.

But my fellow inmates would fashion their modish goatees and mustaches into something very precise, then sculpt their hair styles into quite creative forms. Some of these amateur beauticians were quite ugly, but if beauty is in the eye of the beholder, then it's all relative. Prison existence is dehumanizing, so I think it was the guy's attempt to be unique, to personalize a very impersonal and forced way of semi-living.

Still it was ego-tripping, as pathetic as it was. We were not letting go of that grain of wheat representing our over-bloated sense of selves, to let that ego die, so as to let our real selves bloom into a variety of self expressions, or as Jesus put it, "to produce much fruit." —The OD, Atwater Penitentiary, March 9, 2003

From Disfiguration to Transfiguration
—2nd Sunday Lent 3/16/03

Transfiguration of Jesus—an un-forfeited moment in the life of Peter, James, and John. Can you imagine the WOW coming out of their slack jaws? Later they talked about it a lot—like "we were there"—but only after the temple priests had the Romans execute Jesus. After that hideous dis-figuration, the man rose whole again beautifully transfigured . . . This time permanently.

Transfigured—its root word, figure, is quite familiar in everyday usage in many different ways. As with a beautiful woman, quite a figure! That resident in the White House, go figure! What's the square footage of this church? Figure it out. Art is the portrayal of figures. Its opposite, dis-figure is a distortion of a structure. The Hunchback of Notre Dame, a repulsive figure. The Phantom of the Opera masked the ugly side of his face. Saddam Hussein was cartooned mercilessly. One's enemy is characterized in as distorted a manner as the imagination can picture.

Any figure is a structure. A trans-figuration is a change in that structure for the better. As is a dis-figuration of harmony. The Bushites wanted to further disfigure a city. The stark poverty in those antihuman pig-sties are pits that fester with rage and terror in those neighborhoods, driven to escape into the drug and alcohol culture. This blight disfigures the souls of the wretched who exist there.